2022 WATER TIGER YEAR
Feng Shui and Chinese Astrology

Your destiny is in your hands. Make the most out of it.
Michele Castle

The world is undergoing rapid changes and if the past few years were of any indication; it's not slowing down anytime soon. It is all too human to resist change, to stay in the comfort zone and avoid the great unknown. However, these things don't last. It's only a matter of time before the passage of time irrevocably changes what's familiar to you; that is certain.

But, inevitable as they might be, changes are not always scary and unwelcomed. In fact, it's an opportunity to challenge the status quo and emerge better than when you began. What this guide seeks to accomplish is to give you the insights and inspiration that you need to best prepare in terms of both opportunities and challenges that may come your way.

Among other things, this book contains a wealth of information from the perspective of Feng Shui and Chinese Astrogy. By being conscious and aware of what's happening around you, it will lead you to the outcomes that you want. Even in your most uncertain moments, the transition to the year of the Water Tiger is a certainty. Anticipate what's ahead using these tools and you will find yourself living an inspired life in 2022.

Michele

2022 WATER TIGER YEAR: Feng Shui and Chinese Astrology

Published by Complete Feng Shui
Mb: 0421 116 799,
Email: info@completefengshui.com.au
Website: www.completefengshui.com

2022 WATER TIGER YEAR: Feng Shui and Chinese Astrology©
Text copyright© Michele Castle Illustrations copyright© Michele Castle

All rights reserved. No part of this publication may be reproduced, stored in a retrieval system or transmitted in any form, or by any means, electronic, mechanical, photocopying, recording, or otherwise, without the prior written permission from Complete Feng Shui.

The moral right of the author to be identified as the author of this book has been asserted.

Author: Michele Castle
Design copyright @ Complete Feng Shui
Title: 2022 Water Tiger Year Feng Shui and Chinese Astrology

ISBN-13: 978-06452137-8-2 (Paperback)
ISBN-13: 978-06452137-9-9 (eBook)
May 2022

This Book has been written to offer insight and planning for 2022 energies for Flying Stars, Bagua and Chinese astrology. The author editor and publisher take no responsibility for the outcome of any information implemented from this Book.

The information in this Book is summarized using Flying Star, Bagua and Bazi Formulation as per the Chinese Thousand Year Calendar, presented for you in a user-friendly way to help you enjoy prosperity throughout the year.

Platinum member of the Association of Feng Shui Consultants (AFSC)
Recognised Feng Shui training institution by the (AFSC)

facebook@completefengshui   instagram@completefengshui

Book Cover, Book Layout & eBook Conversion by manuscript2ebook.com

CONTENTS

2022 WATER TIGER YEAR 28

What are the most compatible Chinese Animal Signs with Tiger? 31

WHAT COLOUR CLOTHES SHOULD I WEAR
TO BE IN FENG SHUI FASHION FOR 2022? 54

12 Chinese Astrology Animals & Elements For 2022 59

HOW DOES FOUR PILLARS OF DESTINY or BAZI HELP YOU? 60

SELF-ELEMENT ANALYSIS FOR 2022 62

SELF-ELEMENT Water 2022 65

SELF-ELEMENT Wood 2022 66

SELF-ELEMENT Fire 2022 67

SELF-ELEMENT EARTH 2022 68

SELF-ELEMENT Metal 2022 70

ANIMAL RELATIONSHIPS 71

DID YOU KNOW YOU ARE MORE THAN YOUR ANIMAL SIGN? 72
THRIVING AND SURVIVING IN 2022 73
Do You have AN Abundance of wealth opportunities in 2022? 75
ARE YOU MOST LIKELY TO STEP UP AND SUCCEED in 2022? 76
2022 POWER OF THE SPOKEN WORD – THE VOICE 77
ACADEMIC LEARNING STAR 77
LEADERSHIP IN 2022 77
PROSPERITY STAR 78
THRIVING and SURVIVING IN 2022… YES OR NO TO A NEW JOB! 79
POPULARITY STARS OF 2022 80
ROBOCOP STAR 80
Great Expectations 81
24 MOUNTAIN STARS CHINESE ASTROLOGY ANIMAL INFLUENCES 82
ANIMAL INFLUENCES 2022 BRIEF 88
RAT (1924, 1936, 1948, 1960, 1972, 1984, 1996, 2008, 2020) 89
OX (1925, 1937, 1949, 1961, 1973, 1985, 1997, 2009, 2021) 92
TIGER (1926, 1938, 1950, 1962, 1974, 1986, 1998, 2010, 2022) 95
RABBIT (1915, 1927, 1939, 1951, 1963, 1975, 1987, 1999, 2011) 98
DRAGON (1916, 1928, 1940, 1952, 1964, 1976, 1988, 2000, 2012) 101
SNAKE (1917, 1929, 1941, 1953, 1965, 1977, 1989, 2001, 2013) 103
HORSE (1918, 1930, 1942, 1954, 1966, 1978, 1990, 2002. 2014) 107
GOAT (1919, 1931, 1943, 1955, 1967, 1979, 1991, 2003, 2015) 110
MONKEY (1920, 1932, 1944, 1956, 1968, 1980, 1992, 2004, 2016) 113
ROOSTER (1921, 1933, 1945, 1957, 1969, 1981, 1993, 2005, 2017) 116

DOG (1922, 1934, 1946, 1958, 1970, 1982, 1994, 2006, 2018) 119

PIG (1923, 1935, 1947, 1959, 1971, 1983 1995, 2007, 2019) 122

Annual Flying Stars 125

Compass Reading 132

Identify Your Goals for 2022 138

NORTH Front entrance Annual Visiting Flying Star 1 144

SOUTHWEST Front entrance Annual Visiting Flying Star 2 148

EAST Front Entrance - Annual Visiting Flying Star 3 152

SOUTHEAST Front Entrance -Annual Visiting Flying Star 4......................156

CENTRE Annual Visiting Flying Star 5 160

NORTHWEST Front Entrance -Annual Visiting Flying Star 6....................164

WEST Front Entrance - Annual Visiting Flying Star 7 168

NORTHEAST Front Entrance Annual Visiting Flying Star 8.......................172

SOUTH Front Entrance Annual Visiting Flying Star 9 176

How to Make Salt Water Cure 178

Annual Visiting Flying Star Afflictions 181

Ho Tu Specials 2022 185

Bagua 2022 190

Glossary 195

Candle Space Clearing 200

BEGINNERS FENG SHUI 201

ABOUT Michele Castle..203

WHY MICHELE IS SO ENTHUSIASTIC ABOUT FENG SHUI...

You may ask what led a young mum of three towards such an obscure field. A roller coaster comes to mind as a perfect description: "Any phenomenon, period, or experience of persistent or violent ups and downs, as one fluctuating between prosperity and recession or elation and despair."

Perth will always be home to me. I was raised by a builder and lived in Belair, Cobar, Bowen, and Echuca. Moving around meant that I experienced many different housing arrangements. I went from the prestigious Belair to a home on stilts that rocked at the front with movement.

One home stood out amongst the lot: the home of my Aunty Nikki. Working in a furniture shop in affluent Subiaco, her home décor was bursting with patterns, fabrics, and textures. I wanted one just like it and aspired to be in the realm of Interior Design. I studied the profession, which led to architectural drafting. Fascinated by the impact that design elements played within a home, I started analysing my life and the countless houses I had once called home, looking at the shift in life and luck while in each household.

More than twenty years ago, Feng Shui was brought to my attention as it rapidly gained momentum and interest in the west. Like many, I read about the subject. Friends had their homes healed and my curiosity flourished. A Feng Shui consultant came to my home with a pen in hand and I followed her around as she instructed on colours, furniture placement, and an assortment of symbolism. Red needed to be removed from a wall, furniture directions needed adjustment, Jade and Cumquat plants were to be placed at doors, mirrors, and pictures re-homed, salt went in certain spots, and even crystals hung to redirect energy. The list went on. The thought of a change in luck stimulated my interest and desire. I was in a tailspin – amazed. This was an exciting new venture, a great excuse for an upskill, and unbeknown to me, also a change in my life direction.

I am the Chinese Zodiac animal Rooster and so I needed to understand WHY I could not have a particular wall red, WHY I needed to place salt and crystals in certain pockets, and WHY was I affected by mirrors or the symbolism of artwork. There were a lot of WHYs and so my Feng Shui journey started. I began reading any books relating to the topic that I could get my hands on. Every wall was painted and furniture textures, colours and placements were altered to follow Feng Shui principles. My home was warm and inviting with lots of energy and light. It looked and felt great. My sister and friends liked the energy and requested I help them achieve similar outcomes. With that, my journey escalated. I began investing in courses under well-recognised Feng Shui masters. I wanted to really understand the many levels and influence of energy that was Feng Shui: the Art of placement and manipulation of energy. Feng Shui as an art just clicked; being mathematical, analytical, and practical, it made sense to me.

I loved my hills home, which taught me so much about Feng Shui, energy, and relationships, but that was only the start. Since then, I have successfully navigated the Feng Shui industry for over twenty years, mastering a deep understanding of the multi-layered science of practice.

I have taught Feng Shui, Chinese Astrology, and Metaphysical Studies for Silk Road's Asian Studies at Curtin University and worked with emerging businesses and established enterprises extensively on interiors, renovations. Through many years of practising and consulting, I have become an author, teacher, blogger and public speaker.

HOW DOES FENG SHUI WORK?

Feng Shui and symbolism, the art of placement and the study of energy, can benefit many people. The more you understand, the more you can help yourself. However, just because you have, and practice good Feng Shui does not necessarily mean terrible things will not sometimes happen! However, you will be better protected.

Your Chinese astrology and *Bazi*, or "Four Pillars of Destiny" charts, will determine how you perform and are impacted from year to year. Always remember to do the right thing and stay within your values and morals. Let karma take care of the rest.

How do you explain Feng Shui in a sentence?

"The Feng Shui system is developed and refined based on elements of astronomy, astrology, geology, mathematics, philosophy, psychology, physics, and divination (intuition)."

Three factors make an impact on your life. These factors are:

- Heaven Luck.
- Man Luck; and
- Earth Luck

Words of wisdom from a grandmaster:

An old wise man said:

*"Heaven luck is the boat given to you by God.
Earth luck is the wind that fills the sails and the currents of the ocean.
Human luck is the way in which you use the wind and the currents to steer your boat."*

Meaning:

*Heaven luck is your destiny, Earth luck is Feng Shui to smooth the path that brings opportunities, and Human luck is "You" and how you can shape your path, destiny, and make use of your opportunities.
These are the components of the cosmic Trinity of Luck.*

Your life is always influenced by these three factors. Understanding and mastering the aspects and influences within your environment can have a profound impact on how your influence and performance from one year to the next.

Heaven Luck is the hand you are dealt. It is what is given to you, not by your choosing, but by the energies and forces beyond your control from your date of birth. This is your Bazi or Four Pillars of Destiny chart.

Man, Luck is classified as FREE will and the conscious decisions you make. This includes how you spend your time and which improvements you choose to make

in your life. Knowledge, influence, and education empower you to strengthen your man luck and abilities.

Earth Luck is the modern science and our environment. It includes the people we hang out with, or the buildings in which we live or work from. These would be classed as Feng Shui influences.

Based on the cosmic trinity, you can blueprint your life and year ahead by paying special attention to your Man Luck, the aspects and influences in your life and environment; Heaven Luck, the element and animal forecast from your *Bazi*, or Four Pillars of Destiny chart, understand your capabilities, strengths, weaknesses and opportunities; and Earth luck, the Feng Shui or flying stars of your home, environment, and the world around you.

The next element is understanding timing and the significant impact it has on our results/aspirations and ACTION. Simply put, "FATE is when the girl of your dreams walks into the room. DESTINY is whether you decide to approach her or not." Your life and choices are always about the actions you take or do not.

The wonderful thing about Feng Shui is the positive benefits it can create for everyone. Feng Shui is not just about becoming wealthy or achieving success – it is concerned with enriching lives, reducing aggravations, and bringing happiness into relationships. It is about feeling happy, prosperous, and contented.

When you know how to orient your doors, organise the layout of rooms, arrange furniture, incorporate the use of colours, shapes, and materials, and know about the placement of decorative items in your home, you will discover a new energy and zest for life. Life will become joyous and your relationships with loved ones will reach a stronger levels of understanding. Interactions with others living in the home will begin to improve too!

If you also know how to keep your Feng Shui up to date from year to year, the benefits will be even greater. When your home exhibits good Feng Shui, it literally becomes infused with harmonious energy and an atmosphere of general health. Your home, now happy and calm, will become a real haven – just as a home should be!

Feng Shui is easily applied. The main rule is to keep the Chi (life force energy) moving – never let it stagnate or become unbalanced. Sound, activity, movement, and people all keep Chi in motion. When a space stays too still and is neglected for a period, it stops. However, the simple act of moving the furniture and using different areas of your home will shift the energy, making you feel much better.

The arrangement of our home space is something many of us take for granted. Often, we focus our attention purely on the aesthetic of arrangement and décor. Insufficient consideration is given to Feng Shui design implications. Correct Feng Shui inputs can improve the luck of almost every home, irrespective of style or decoration.

At worst, bad Feng Shui and negative elements lead to anger, loss, and even violence. Bad Feng Shui means negatives are present, causing many problems such as health issues and monetary loss. If the cause of bad energy is not addressed, you will continue to suffer challenging times.

TIME AFFLICTIONS

The other aspect of Feng Shui that must be accounted for is time. While *physical afflictions* are the result of placement (design, blockages and orientation), *time afflictions* are caused by the passing of time. Therefore, we have two dimensions that influence Feng Shui: space and time. To ensure that you make the best of *time energy*, you need to update your Feng Shui in accordance with changing time.

The Chinese place great emphasis on the calendar. The main Chinese calendar is the lunar calendar. Each cycle of calendar time is expressed in terms of the Five Elements: Fire, Earth, Metal, Water and Wood. These Five Elements, combined with the twelve animals, make a major cycle that lasts for sixty years.

As we move from one year to the next, energy changes, transforming from Yin to Yang, from element to element, and from one animal sign to the next. Depending on the ruling element and animal from one month to the next, the energy in the home and its resident's change. Time exerts a very strong impact on your Feng Shui, luck, and destiny.

Good Feng Shui cannot and does not last forever. It must be recharged with small but significant changes every year. Energy must be refreshed, reorganised, and rejuvenated; spaces and places need maintenance and energy must keep moving.

The Flying Stars formula of Feng Shui is a technical approach that directly addresses the effect of time on the energy of homes and businesses.

You can tell from month to month where illness energy lingers. This can be suppressed with remedies. Most importantly, you can stop monetary loss, broken relationships, frustration, disharmony, and the pernicious effect of aggravating people with the correct application of cures and enhancers.

By investing the time and effort of Feng Shui in your home, you will have added a valuable resource to your life. After enhancing the energy of your surroundings with Feng Shui, your view and approach to living spaces will never be the same again.

With the understanding of Feng Shui, you can develop an increased sensitivity to the environment around you, with this awareness will come respect for your surroundings. You do not have to "believe" in Feng Shui for it to work, Feng Shui is always all around you...

GENERAL OUTLOOK
2022 WATER TIGER YEAR

2022 WATER TIGER YEAR

Chinese Metaphysical studies work from the Chinese Calendar, also known as the "farmer's calendar" or the "Hsia calendar." The Chinese Calendar is a uniquely accurate system where everything in the Universe is represented by the Five Elements:

- Metal
- Water
- Wood
- Fire
- Earth

The relationship between these five elements helps to predict what is happening worldwide and within people's destinies. Every person has a combination of all these elements present in their birth chart - known as *Bazi*, or "Four Pillars of Destiny." The elements' presence gives insight into a person's destiny. They interact with each other either positively or negatively, which either forms good or bad relationships, health or health issues, success or struggle, and so forth. From there, you can analyse a person's destiny based on his or her birth date and better understand and accurately predict the cycles of a person's fortune. In so doing, you can learn how to multiply the good luck or minimize the bad luck in life.

Additionally, the relationships of the Chinese Five Elements are believed to be the basic components of everything in the universe, including sounds, colours, shapes, directions, numbers, emotions, organs… the list goes on. Therefore, when you begin to understand the sophisticated relationships of the Five Elements, you can say that you have a greater understanding of the theory of life.

The interaction is classified into three cycles:

1. Productive Cycle
2. Exhaustive Cycle
3. Destructive Cycle

The elements are either favourable, producing positive things for each other, or they are unfavourable, and they exhaust or destroy us. The Earth also has a *Bazi* chart, which changes each year as it is derived from the elements present per the date.

In the Hsia calendar, 2022 is symbolized by two Chinese characters: **Yang Water** sitting on top of **Wood Tiger**. Yang Water is the Heavenly Stem (the character on the top), and the Tiger is the Earthly Branch (the character on the bottom). In the Five Elements cycle, Water gives birth to Wood.

According to the cycle of birth and destruction, if the two elements are in the birth cycle and have a supportive relationship, then the year will have more harmony. The 2022 Water - Wood elements configuration in a supportive cycle will help to resolve conflict and bring more harmony in international relationships. However, the Yang water on top represents fierce ocean water, which sometimes becomes a tsunami. This may trigger impulsive and fierce violent actions without careful consideration and planning.

It is likely there could still be skirmishes and conflicts, or even war and destructive actions, but it appears the Water Tiger year will be positive and productive, leading toward peace, healing, and recovery.

Qualities of Yang Water

Let us explore the nature of this year's Heavenly Stem and Earthly Branch. Though they do come together in a supportive relationship, do not be fooled as the characteristic of Yang Water is quite powerful.

Yang Water symbolises a powerful ocean water. It is also representing intelligence, enthusiasm, devotion, and pioneering. As such, it is associated with positive drive and innovative ideas. A person born on a Yang Water Day often appears to be energetic, aggressive like an ocean and full of drive and passion to achieve their goals. On the outside, they can sometimes behave harsh, impatient and impulsive. However, water is by nature a powerful and intelligent element, so Yang Water people often possess strong intelligence, enthusiasm, devotion, and leadership ability.

They are usually masculine, powerful, straightforward, and forceful types of people. A typical Yang Water person is Bill Gates. He is energetic, intelligent, and innovative. Not only is he a successful business leader, but also a generous philanthropist.

Other famous Yang Water celebrities include Tom Cruise, Jimmy Page, Paul McCartney, Prince Harry, Anthony Hopkins, and Warren Buffet. Yang Water ladies are equally charming and successful, with examples such as Kate Middleton, the US Vice-President Kamala Harris, Jennifer Lawrence, and Joan Jett.

Qualities of the Tiger

Rash, impulsive, and dynamic, Tigers don't know how to sit still. They take fearsome risks but make good heroes. Tigers like to champion the underdog and will fight against any injustice. They are invariably charming and persuasive leaders, not because of any natural leading abilities, but because they can talk anyone into following them – no matter how ill-advised the project may be.

The Tiger is one of the most tenacious characters in the Chinese Zodiac and very little will daunt Tigers or keep them down for long. However, Tigers still have vulnerabilities and need lots of emotional support to compensate for their insecurities and feelings of not being loved.

Tigers have infinite resources of energy and imagination that will inevitably tire any lover they tangle with. They are promiscuous and have absolutely no morals whatsoever, with no compunction about finding new excitement once the current relationship has begun to fade. They are great romantics and fall in love easily and often. They do have a great capacity for intense relationships and are devastated when these fall apart, even if they are the cause. A Tiger in love can go rogue or simply perfect and you won't know which sort you're getting until it's too late.

Tigers are loners with few good friends, but those they do have, they keep for life. They make good parents, not because they set good examples, but because children adore these exciting and charismatic personalities. They can be very strict and demanding, tending to expect a lot from their offspring. In business, Tigers are adventurous speculators, full of ideas. They are good at starting new projects with enthusiasm and energy, but they hate routine and get bored easily.

The Tiger is... **Best with** Pig, Rabbit, Horse, Ox, and Dog.
And **Worst with** Monkey and Snake.

What are the most compatible Chinese Animal Signs with Tiger?

The most compatible Chinese Animal Signs for Tiger are the Pig, Rabbit, Horse, and Ox. Tigers have a love relationship with Pigs in the Chinese Horoscopes. Tigers and Horses have an attractive relationship because of Fire. The Horse is a most trustworthy and reliable partner for the Tiger. Tigers and Rabbits have an attractive relationship because of Wood. Rabbits like to follow the leader, the Tiger. Tigers and Ox have hidden love relationships.

What are the most incompatible Chinese Animal Signs with Tiger?

Tigers and Monkeys have a fighting relationship in the Chinese Horoscopes. Monkeys are not a reliable partner for Tigers. Tigers and Snakes are strong rivals in competition. The Snake will have continuous conflicts with the Tiger without resolutions.

Four Pillars of Destiny

People born in the Year of the Tiger (1926,1938, 1950, 1962, 1974, 1986, 1998, 2010, 2022) are said to be "offending the Grand Duke." This means you are offending the energy of the year. Therefore, it is recommended to carry a pendant of the Pig to reduce the negative influence.

Famous people who are offending the Tiger Year include Tom Cruise, Martin Short, Pamela Stephenson, Richard Branson, William Hurt, Queen Elizabeth II, Leonardo DiCaprio, Ed Harris, Emilio Estevez, Joaquin Phoenix, Jane Pauley, Demi Moore, Jodie Foster, Penelope Cruz, Kenny Rogers, Lady Gaga, and Victoria Beckham.

The animal sign that is most unfavourable to the Tiger is the Monkey. If you were born in the Year of the Monkey (1920, 1932, 1944, 1956, 1968, 1980, 1992, 2004, 2016), you are in direct clash with this year. Clashes will bring turbulence, movements, accidents, or even big changes. You can anticipate more travelling opportunities and it is a good year to change jobs or move offices or houses. You must carry the Pig pendant for protection and refrain from participating in risky sports such as driving fast cars, piloting aeroplanes, skydiving, or parachuting.

Famous people born in the Year of the Monkey include Dave Grohl, Chris Isaak, Jessica Simpson, Will Smith, Owen Wilson, Macaulay Culbin, Rod Stewart, Lisa Marie Presley, Daniel Craig, Justin Timberlake, Celine Dion, and Hugh Jackman.

You can also be clashing if you were not born in the Monkey Year if you were born on the Monkey Day. Examples include Mark Zuckerberg, Jeff Bezos, Elon Musk, and David Beckham. The clash is even more severe in this case and you could face a challenging year ahead. This clash can also adversely impact your relationship with a spouse or someone of the opposite sex. The celestial animals that combine with the Tiger are the Pig, Horse, and Dog. These animals are in a year of harmony.

2022 OVERVIEW

The Tiger is the animal in clash against the Monkey. It is a clash between Wood and Metal land animals and they are travelling stars. This will trigger traffic accidents so there will be more car, train, and aeroplane crashes. The Tiger is the birthplace of fire and is strong in stimulating explosions and fire disasters. In the human body, fire represents blood circulation and the heart, so it is a year with more inflammation and heart and blood diseases.

People born in a year of the Monkey are in clash against the year. They usually have more movements and travelling in 2022. it is okay to take chances to make necessary changes, such as moving house, moving office, changing job, or taking trips. However, the Monkey should take extra care. For people born in a year of the Monkey, it is good to minimise travelling directly towards the northeast direction, as it is the direction of the Grand Duke in 2022.

In the system of Four Pillars of Destiny, the Tiger is part of the "Three Fire Penalty." When the Tiger encounters the Snake and the Monkey, it will create a massive amount of Fire element. If it is an unfavourable element to a person, he will encounter trouble related to fire, which may range from bad relationships and legal trouble to blood and heart problems, inflammation, or even fire disaster.

An example of people who have died from the Tiger - Snake - Monkey penalty is the famous King of Rock and Roll, Elvis Presley, who collapsed at home on 16 August 1977 from heart disease and inflammation problems. This occurred during a Snake year, Monkey Month, Snake Day, and Monkey hour. Elvis was born at an Hour of the Tiger, creating the Tiger Snake Monkey fire penalty.

Another example is Tom Cruise, who was born in a year of Tiger, a day of Water Tiger, at the hour of Monkey, so when the Snake year arrives, he will suffer from Tiger - Snake - Monkey penalty, which affects his day pillar – the House of Spouse. He divorced Nicole Kidman in the Snake year of 2001, and again divorced Katie Holmes in the Snake year of 2013.

Michael Schumacher was born in a Monkey Year and Tiger Day and he had an accident when skiing in Snake year 2013, on the day of Snake, and at the hour of Snake. Such Fire penalty caused serious bleeding in his brain.

In 2022, some celebrities have Tiger - Snake - Monkey penalties in their chart. Examples include Bob Dylan, Mark Zuckerberg, Emperor Naruhito, and Roman Polanski.

Another example of Tiger - Snake - Monkey penalty can be said to have caused the explosion in the 1986 Challenger space shuttle during take-off. It was Fire Tiger Year, on Horse Day and Snake Hour, and one of the famous victims in the disaster was Christa McAuliffe, who was born in Monkey month and Tiger Day. The tragedy happened during her luck pillar of Snake. In the same Tiger Year of 1986 was the famous Chernobyl nuclear disaster. Also, the Japanese 311 tsunami-triggered explosion at the Fukushima nuclear station was on 12 March 2011, which is also a fire Tiger Day.

The Sexagenary Cycle

As you learn more about the Hsia calendar and the system of the Four Pillars of Destiny, you will understand that everything is in a repeating, sixty-year cycle (120, 180, 240, etc.). All you need do is simply look back and revisit history to learn about the future. For example, sixty years ago in 1962, it was a Yang Water Tiger Year. This was a significant year, as the world entered a phase of serious global tensions between the United States and the USSR.

Because of the Fire Element's absence, the powerful Water Element from 2021 will continue into 2022. This will cause more Water (sea) and Fire (air) disasters. It is bleak, but on the upside, we can expect 2022 to bring us a year of movement and growth.

The Tiger is also a powerful "Travelling Star," which will trigger international travelling, with tourism and airline business returning to normal. This should be the most important aspect of 2022, meaning the pandemic is under control and the world starts moving again.

However, a "Travelling Horse" can also be triggered from frequent movements and travelling traffic accidents. As the Tiger is a land animal, in the past it is believed that accidents are more related to cars and land traffic. But if we look back to 1962, it seems there were plenty of air traffic accidents as well:

- American Airlines aeroplane crashed during take-off at New York on 1st March 1962.
- US military aircraft vanished 16th March over the Western Pacific Ocean.
- On the 22nd of May, a Continental Airlines plane crashed in Missouri.
- Air France plane crashed during take-off in Paris on the 3rd of June.

There are also plenty of train accidents recorded in 1962:

- In Japan, on the 3rd of May, there was a train crash in Tokyo.
- The worst Dutch train disaster occurred in January.

2022 being a Water and Wood year, the Earth element becomes relatively weak, creating the likelihood of earth disasters. Sixty years ago, on the 10th of Jan 1962, there was an avalanche in Peru. There was also a coal mine explosion in West Germany on the 7th of February and a serious mine fire in Pennsylvania on the 27th of May. A coal mining disaster occurred in Norway on the 5th of November.

You may notice these are underground fire or explosion disasters and the Fire is hidden inside the Tiger in the Earthly Branch. Incidents are also occurring in the Snake month, also a travel star.

With the drastic and aggressive character of Yang water, there is still a tendency toward conflict, tension, and terrorist attacks. In 1962, there was a Cuban missile crisis, which almost triggered a nuclear war between USSR and the USA. There were border conflicts between China and India, and in 1842, 180 years ago, it was the end of the Opium War between Britain and China, resulting in the signing of the Treaty of Nanking on 29th August.

Tiger combining with Horse and Dog will create a big Fire element. This means there will be a greater chance of fire disasters and explosions during a Tiger year. This can also have an impact on one's health. 2022 is a triple Tiger year, so if Fire is not a favourable element to a person's four pillars, such a strong configuration of fire may trigger heart and blood problems.

Examples of such Tiger – Horse - Dog combination will occur to some celebrities, such as Donald Trump, President George Bush, Paris Hilton, and Sylvester Stallone.

2022 brings Academic Star

Yang Water sitting on Tiger is described as "Academic Star" in the system of "Four Pillars of Destiny." Academic Star is a symbol of intelligence and intellectual ability.

People who possess such a star in their birth chart may not get high grades at school, but they are keen to explore and absorb knowledge that interests them. Therefore, they will be successful in the field that they find interesting. Such people include Albert Einstein, Mark Zuckerberg, Beethoven, Vincent Van Gogh, and Stephen King. All babies born in 2022 automatically possess Academic Star Tiger in their birth year. This is a particularly beneficial quality in the modern world when high-tech business based on knowledge is of paramount importance.

The Water Tiger year, with Water producing Wood, also symbolize creativity and growth which injects a lot of creative activities into art. The Tiger Academic Star not only supports culture, art, and science, but also stimulating entertainment and restaurant businesses. Many celebrity cooks, such as Jamie Oliver and Maria Cordero, also possess Academic Star as cooking is also an intellectual art.

Health

In Traditional Chinese Medicine ("TCM"), the Wood element represents the liver. It is also responsible for the growth, activities, and motion of our limbs, meaning there will be more of a tendency for people to be active. The Water element is related to the kidneys, urinary system, and sex organs. With such Water sitting on Wood, Water becomes drained and weak, so it is necessary to take care to support the water aspects.

The weakness of Fire means the Fire organs are also impacted. These include the heart, blood circulation, and overall vitality of the body. The excessive amount of Water this year could wreak havoc on the urinary system, kidneys, and reproductive organs. Both Water and Wood are against Earth, which is our stomach and digestion system. You should support Earth with more antioxidants to regulate our earth element, which also refers to our cells.

Stock Market and Economic Outlook

In the Five Elements system, Fire is happiness and optimism, which prevailed in the years of Fire from 2013 to 2017. 2020 brought the Water element, but the Fire energy was totally absent. The global disaster of COVID-19 cast the dark shadow of fear all over the world. In 2021 we continued to be under strong Water influence and the atmosphere remained dull, cold, and grey. In 2022, the Water Tiger gives life to Wood, bringing growth and creating optimism that will enable economic recovery. 2022 will be a year of resuming business and travelling the world after two gloomy years. The Wood element symbolizes growth and activities, so economic growth will return, and the stock market will become very active.

Luck of the Different Industries in 2022

The Water Wood element of 2022 is expected to bring prosperity to Metal industries and Earth industries. This is because Metal conquers Wood, so the Wood element is a symbol of money to Metal industries, which includes banking, high-tech, car, machinery, engineering, beauty, and skincare.

The second-best industries could be Earth, as Earth conquers Water. Water means money to the Earth industry. Earth industries include property, mining, insurance, and computer software.

Water industry sees Wood as productivity, so Water industries will also benefit from the growth and moving nature of Wood. Water industries are communication, transport, and shipping.

Wood industry is facing serious competition. Wood industries include textile, media, papers, and magazines.

Fire industry is not making money in a Tiger year as there is a total absence of Metal, which is their money.

In summary, the industries that will perform better in the year of the Tiger will be industries related to the Metal element and the Earth element. The other industries of Fire and Wood will not have such a prosperous year in 2022.

In general, the Yang Water Tiger year with Yang Water on top and Wood Tiger below, is a symbol of creativity, growth, movement, and travelling. There will be good recovery from the dormant atmosphere of 2020 and 2021.

Global Outlook

Fire's presence can boost people's confidence in the economy and consequently, promote good performance in the stock market. This was the main driving force behind the stock market boom in those years. However, the cycle of the Fire Element ended in 2017 with Yin Fire Rooster. When the Dog Year arrived in 2018, Fire entered the grave, resulting in a setback of the economic atmosphere and creating a lacklustre, zero-sum year. Then, the Year of the Yin Earth Pig in 2019 represented the termination of the Fire Element. The pessimism of the Water energy - the symbolic emotion related to fear - had begun. Hence, the world economy has been greatly affected by the trade war talks between the U.S. and China, which generated a lot of fear and uncertainty for global investors.

The years 2019 to 2021 all belong to the Water and Metal Elements and the Fire Element will not return until the year 2025. Because 2019 represented the termination of Fire, 2020 meant that Fire entered the embryo stage. Finally, in 2021, Fire moved into the nourishing cycle, and therefore the general economic atmosphere is mostly bearish with the economic pace gloomy and slow in 2021.

2022 brings action, movement, and growth. As the world economy recovers, there will be more joyful sentiments, bringing back entertainment and travelling, which was almost totally absent under COVID-19 in the last two years. There are still international tension and social unrest as people are in a liberal mood with more desire to make changes.

The Tiger is not a peaceful animal and Wood is often associated with Wind. Therefore, we can expect stormy weather. In previous Yang Water - Wood - Tiger years, there were plenty of weather-related disasters. Severe typhoons, heavy storm flooding, flash floods, big storms, and even a big freeze all occurred in 1962. Natural disasters such as earthquakes, landslides, sea and air accidents, environmental disasters, and world epidemics will continue to persist and prevail.

Other

There are a few interesting things to point out about today's world leaders. Tiger and Wood are favourable elements to President Biden, so he will be more stable in his second year of presidency. However, Donald Trump must face a Tiger – Horse - Dog Fire combination, which is not his favourable element. Donald Trump will find he has obstacles that reduce his chance of running for president a second time.

Putin is extremely weak Fire and does not like Wood, so the Tiger Year will bring some trouble to Russia. In China, the Tiger is not a very favourable element to Xi Jinping, so there will be obstacles, but he is still in strong favourable noblemen luck. Wood is also supportive of the big, high-tech businesses in China, so China will still lead in the economic recovery.

IMPORTANT INDICATIONS FOR 2022

Relationship Luck

Marriage luck is weak, with plenty of temptation.

Avoid jumping to conclusions. Toxic energy creates misunderstandings.

Beware of smooth talkers with the "gift of the gab".

Tiger brings jealousy and suspicion, which is why communication is key.

Betrayal and infidelity energies can tip the scales in rocky relationships.

Health Luck

Health luck is weak, especially for matriarchs.

Expect ailments and allergies to be more pronounced.

Homes built on SW-NE axis must take extra care.

Strong remedies needed to overcome illness afflictions.

To keep healthy, sleep before Hour of the Rat and get ample exercise.

Education Luck

Distractions abound. Make it a point to stay focused.

Do not let emotions affect your self-confidence.

Friendships may be afflicted due to increased competitiveness.

A challenging year, but great rewards await the diligent and hardworking.

There are opportunities to take advantage of. Stay attentive to these.

Business and Wealth Luck

Much wealth is to be made in 2022.

2022 a period of strong growth.

Streamline processes and curb unnecessary expenditure as healthy cash reserves are vital.

Beware of enemies appearing as close allies.

Unbalanced annual elements point to conflicts that can lead to great misfortune.

Stock Market Outlook

There is strong growth energy at beginning of the year.

Cash flow problems will affect the second half of the year.

Fire months bring potential profits.

Beware of companies that make overly optimistic announcements.

Innovative firms with new technology continue to grow.

Career Outlook

The year brings new opportunities and career growth.

There are many wolves in sheep's clothing. Do not be too trusting.

Avoid confrontations with co-workers. Stay calm amidst conflict.

Expect to take on more responsibility and workload this year.

EARTH ELEMENT INDUSTRIES

PROPERTY, REAL ESTATE, BUILDING, CONSTRUCTION, HOTELS

- A challenging year with increased competition.

- Lack of financial resources leads to stagnant projects.

- Consolidation of companies improves profits.

- Oversupply threatens profit margins and increases selling costs.

METAL ELEMENT INDUSTRIES

MINING, JEWELLERY, WHITE GOODS, COMPUTER, AIRLINES

- Maintain low overheads as business continues to be poor.
- Consolidate strengths and reduce costs to stay competitive.
- Innovation and new ideas improve market share.
- Very competitive.
- Lack of mentor luck.

WATER ELEMENT INDUSTRIES

BANKING, SHIPPING, TRANSPORT, ALCOHOL, FISHING

- Potential spike in sales during Autumn months.

- Business rivalry and fierce competition will create obstacles

- Innovation is key to improved sales.

- Must be nimble and quick to adapt to stay relevant.

WOOD ELEMENT INDUSTRIES

PLANTATION, AGRICULTURE, PUBLISHING FLOWERS, PLANTS

- Overproduction and improved harvests.

- Oversupply and reduced demand will reduce profitability.

- New products and fresh marketing plans needed to improve turnover.

- Be proactive against business rivalry.

FIRE ELEMENT INDUSTRIES

STOCK MARKET, ENTERTAINMENT, LIGHTING, RESTAURANTS

- Market remains highly speculative, but there is the potential for growth.

- The year starts and ends on a bearish note.

- The middle portion of the year brings short-lived profits.

- Focus on companies with strong fundamentals.

- New technology and creativity put companies ahead.

WHAT COLOUR CLOTHES SHOULD I WEAR TO BE IN FENG SHUI FASHION FOR 2022?

Did you know Feng Shui can influence your wardrobe as well as your home and surroundings? Fashion can become quite an important and integral part of your life, just like your home remedies.

The tradition to wear specific colours for each coming New Year is based on Chinese metaphysics. There are five main colours which signify the five elements and the five directions – Earth, Metal, Water, Wood and Fire, and the eight directions – North, Northeast, Northwest, South, Southeast, Southwest, East, and West. Different homes have assorted colour affinities and different personalities to vibrate better with certain colours in different years. This dynamic aspect of the use of colours will ensure good fortune.

Since 2022 is a year of the water element (the Water Tiger), it is recommended to wear the colours of the Water Feng Shu elements aqua, blue, black, and charcoal to be in harmony with the energy of the year and befriend the ruling Water Tiger.

BLUE or BLACK improves wealth potential in 2022.

Both blue and black signify flowing water, which brings change and swift communication. The flow of news moves as fast as water flows. Wearing black or blue in 2022 strengthens networking, friendship, but also competition. Due to an

excess of Water in the chart for the year, try to avoid over-using blue or black as you do not want to strengthen gossip and/or betrayals. If you wear a totally black outfit, always balance this out with a colourful bag, lipstick, or a bright scarf and jewellery. Blues and blacks symbolize flowing water which always brings good wealth potential. Moreover, the WATER element in 2022 stands for WEALTH.

Most of the wealth luck in 2022 manifests in "direct form", which means money from doing business or wages from work done. "Indirect wealth" is the kind that comes from investments or speculation and lotteries. This will be featured much less throughout the year.

GREEN brings recognition and fame.

For 2022, the colour green is very auspicious, as green represents intelligence and creativity. Green is also one of the favourable colours of the year. Note that the colour green stands for steady and healthy growth, indicating progress in one's career.

Green is the colour of Wood and because Wood is the element of output in 2022, green is also the colour of success. If you are unwell, sit by a window overlooking gardens as a form of therapy. Green also signifies action, so wearing green will energize you toward action.

The lucky gemstone associated with green is **GREEN JADE**. Green Jade brings great fortune to those who wear it close to their bodies, especially when worn as hand bangles near the pulse points on the hand. As green is so auspicious in 2022, it is extremely beneficial to wear jade in 2022.

RED brings support and resources.

For 2022, the colour red is incredibly lucky as it represents increased incomes and great wealth. This is a year where Fire only appears as a hidden element. The colour red is universally acknowledged as a particularly important and auspicious colour. It is important not to overuse this colour. While wearing red is incredibly lucky indeed, painting the whole house red is quite another matter. When Fire energy becomes excessive, it can turn destructive.

Red is always favoured for the New Year, weddings, and event celebration. Activating the colour red attracts good fortune! It is also the favourite colour of temples and restaurants, as it is believed to be the most powerful colour for attracting customers and clients. In 2022, it is the colour that represents WEALTH luck.

YELLOW represents alliance and friendships.

In 2022, the colour yellow represents friendships, social networking, recognition, power, rank, intelligence, and creativity. This is the colour of Earth, which brings stability and patience. It makes one grounded and realistic. Because Earth is in excess this year, too much of this colour will cause excessive worrying and self-induced stress.

Yellow has always been a noble and high-class colour. The Chinese have always revered this colour, associating it with Imperial Authority since yellow is the colour of the Son of Heaven. Yellow is also the emperor's colour and the colour of the Yellow River, which brings water to the fields of rice and grain.

WHITE brings intelligence and talent.

White is the colour associated with the element Metal, which in 2022 is the element that represents talent, fresh ideas, resources, support, and authority. Anyone working in an environment which requires creative thought will benefit very much from wearing white, gold, and silver since Metal is missing from the 2022 chart. This colour in 2022 also brings original thinking, allowing one to think outside the box to come up with inspired solutions to difficult problems that otherwise seem hard to solve. This is a good colour to wear when you are struggling to come up with new ideas or when you need to think on your feet, such as in interviews, important meetings, or presentations. You can also wear colours associated with the Metal element such as silvery grey and gold. Both metallic colours also represent money, so they are always regarded as auspicious.

12 CHINESE ASTROLOGY ANIMALS & ELEMENTS FOR 2022

HOW DOES FOUR PILLARS OF DESTINY or BAZI HELP YOU?

A Four Pillar of Destiny chart or Bazi chart is the combination of Chinese Astrology animals and elements. Think of Four Pillars of Destiny / Bazi as your very own personal cheat sheet. It is like a guidebook that reveals your thought patterns, greatest talents, and how you can achieve potential and identify opportunities that would come your way. When you are aware of these things, it will help you become the best version of yourself, make better decisions, and live a better life. Understanding how to avoid challenges and pitfalls from one year to the next gives you the ultimate opportunity to overcome any challenges that life serves.

We are all equipped with so much within us to change our futures. We get to decide how our lives turn out and the moves to evoke change. Whether in terms of wealth, relationships, career, or health, every choice we make serves as a preview of what our futures can hold. Along the way, though, we seek guidance from energies of the universe in the hopes that we're more informed on what works best for us.

The exact effect 2022 will have on experiencing either positive or negative energy depends on your personal Four Pillars of Destiny or Bazi chart.

Your Four Pillars of Destiny or Bazi chart is your life's blueprint. All the information is derived from your hour, day, month, and year of birth; and therefore, never changes. The only point of difference in each year is the influence each self-element and animal present in your chart bring to you. The heavenly stems are the top row where you find your SELF-ELEMENT or Day Master, and the bottom row is the earthly branches displayed as the Chinese animals.

You may be a beginner and only know your year of birth Chinese Astrology animal, but if you understand your own personal Four Pillar of Destiny or Bazi chart

It is important to know how the Chinese animals in your chart will affect you, but it is equally important to understand your self-elements and how the year's energies will interact with you. This will enable you to take advantage of prosperity and 'cushion the blow' in times of hardship.

Your self-element is the top element off the day you are born.

Example below the self-element is Yin Metal.

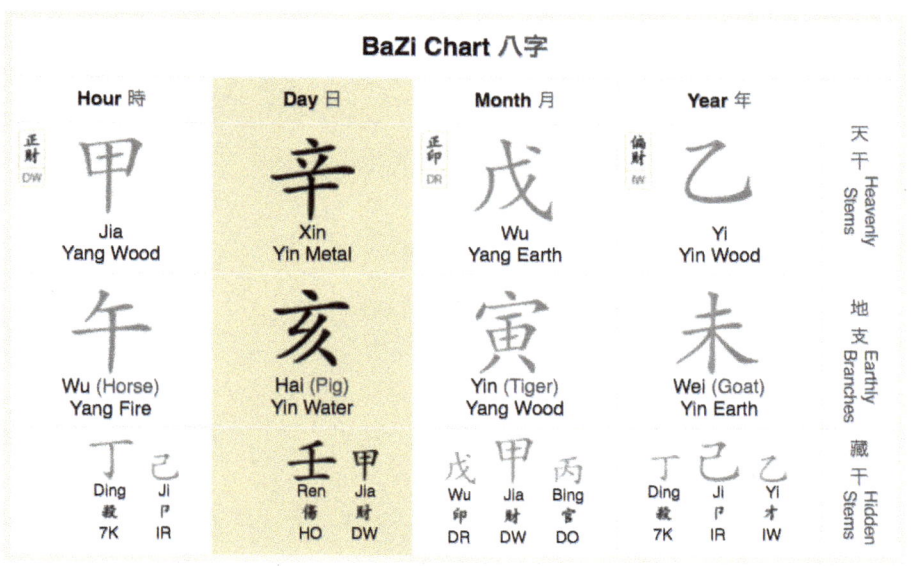

SELF-ELEMENT ANALYSIS FOR 2022

Your SELF-ELEMENT or day master is the element shown in your day pillar on the top heavenly stem of a Four Pillar of Destiny or Bazi chart.

Once you know your Self-element, you can break down your chart further and understand your strongest characteristics. Ask yourself these questions:

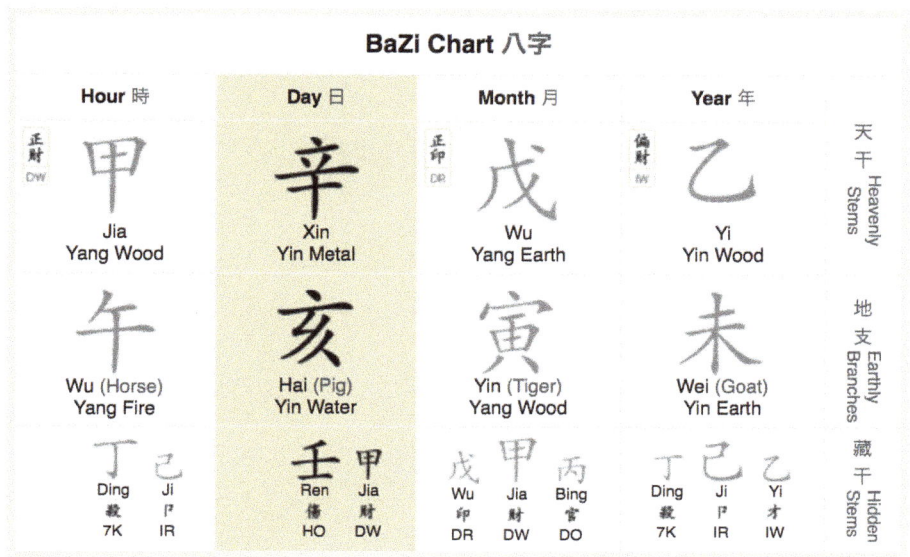

What do you believe is your strongest characteristic?

Which is the strongest element shown within your chart?

Earth Likes to be comfortable and take things easy.

Fire Is competitive and always strives to win.

Wood Values being liked and adored.

Water Strives always to have their wants, freedom, and enjoyment.

Metal Judicious, righteous, and always like to be correct.

Characteristics of Your Self-Element or Day Master...

YANG WOOD Strong and sturdy, Yang Wood can be described as a tall tree. By nature, you are blunt, protective, and straightforward.

YIN WOOD Resilient and flexible, Yin Wood is like the creeping vines. By nature, you are a natural-born survivor, temperamental and cunning.

YANG FIRE Shining bright and full of energy, Yang Fire is the sun itself. By nature, you are inspirational, conservative, and confident.

YIN FIRE Like a flickering candle, Yin Fire is rather mystical. You are a guiding light for others, empathic and sensitive by nature.

YANG EARTH Strong as a mountain, Yang Earth people stand their ground. By nature, you are trustworthy, tough, and resilient.

YIN EARTH Yin Earth is like the fertile soil that nurtures and grows crops. By nature, you are kind, patient, and understanding.

YANG METAL Sharp as a blade and ready to fight, Yang Metal are born warriors. By nature, you are brave, determined, and motivated.

YIN METAL Yin Metal is likened to precious jewellery. By nature, you are rather witty, believe in working smart-not-hard, and crave attention.

YANG WATER Like a deep ocean, Yang Water has strong undercurrents running beneath calm waters. By nature, you are intellectual, eccentric, and mysterious.

YIN WATER Yin Water can be described as the clouds in the sky. By nature, you are carefree, easy-going, and have wanderlust in your heart.

SELF-ELEMENT Water 2022

Yang and Yin are friends/companions and output elements for both Water Day masters. In the year of the Water Tiger, they will attract the attention of those willing to help them out. They cherish those who share a similar mindset.

Yang Water Day Masters will see Yang Water as its friend/companion star. 2022 will be a good year to build social networks. The ability to meet new people, forge new connections, and generate creativity will be a bridge to form some positive values with those around them. The best thing you can do would be to get out of your comfort zone and put yourself out there.

Yang Water is the Rob Wealth Star for Yin Water Day Masters. With this, there will be some unexpected changes happening. Things may appear calm, but still, waters often run deep. Be careful when you speak, for words can cut like a knife. Watch what you say, and do not go around picking fights with others.

How to succeed in 2022

Yang and Yin Water Day masters shouldn't be too laid back when trying moments arise for a good year ahead. Instead, always be prepared for the worst-case scenarios. Sometimes, even peaceful instances may change. At the same time, keep in mind that harmony brings wealth, and being friendly may be the key to success. Trust the timing and know that everything happens when it is meant to. In the meantime, just work hard.

SELF-ELEMENT Wood 2022

Yang Wood Day Masters will see Yang Water as its indirect resource star. Besides that, it is also one of the hidden stems of the Earthly Branch Yin (Tiger). The indirect resource stands for one's instinct and intuition. Being creative with diversifying their income sources is rather good. There will be plenty of opportunities to receive some extra money this year. The road to wealth will be wide, so make sure to take advantage of it.

Meanwhile, Yang Water is the direct resource star for Yin Wood Day Masters. The direct resource brings about analysis skills in general, but more so in being specifically able to hone in on the details. People under this sign will monetize and capitalize on their ideas. However, remember that you should never forego your health, no matter how busy things get.

How to Succeed in 2022

Make plans in 2022, but also try and have a schedule you can abide by. Be calm no matter what life throws at you. It is important to remember that sometimes taking a break could be needed for the bigger picture. Besides that, do go to the doctor when you feel like necessary. This is the only way that you will be able to stay on top of your game.

SELF-ELEMENT Fire 2022

Yang and Yin are the influence and the resource elements for the Fire Day Masters. In 2022, both Yang and Yin will be recognized and gain the power they deserve. They will also have a good plan on how to have things happen for them.

This year, the Yang Fire Day Masters may not be as good as they'd like. This is because Yang Water is the seven killings star. The presence of the seven killings star could be a sign of troubled times. However, do not be disheartened, for it is not without a way out. Yang is one of the hidden stems of the year branch Yin (Tiger). It also has the blessings of the heavenly wealth this year. This means that the Yang people have the answers to their problems within themselves. They are rather excellent at being innovative and thinking outside the box.

Besides, Yang Water is the direct officer star for the Yin Fire Day Masters. This year, career opportunities are available, so do what you must claim them. The direct officer promotes discipline, so use this to make the year one more disciplined and detail oriented. Be outgoing in your pursuits and show the people around you what you're made of.

How to succeed in 2022

A good year in 2022 is learning to prioritize the important things in life. Build bridges instead of burning them down. Be more receptive to others and always put your health as a top priority. Taking care of your well-being is the best form of self-love.

SELF-ELEMENT EARTH 2022

The Yin Earth person is nurturing, highly adaptable, tolerant, productive, and resourceful. They are persistent rather than stubborn and are recognized for their willingness and capability to cope with hardship. Both yin and yang can endure hardship without flinching.

The elements of the Earth Day Masters are wealth and influence. For the year 2022, many of you will get a chance to reach far and wide in your career. It will be a suitable time to make changes to achieve the goals you have set for yourself.

For Yang Earth Day Masters, Yang Water is the indirect wealth star. It will also possess the hidden stems of the year branch Yin (Tiger). Due to those qualities, this lot will see windfall gains throughout the year, and they would crop up rather unexpectedly. However, keep in mind that this does not mean it will come without effort.

When the Yin Earth Day Masters combines with Yang, good relationships with those around you will increase. Besides that, Yang Water is the direct wealth star, so this year a stable income, as well as a rather peaceful life, will grace you. Keep your eyes peeled for any opportunities that surface, for they may bring some favourable results. Do make use of the luck you have.

How to succeed in 2022

A thriving 2022 will be finding the silver linings in problems, finding solutions that have good value, and taking responsibility for your actions. Act consistently and do not opt for any shortcuts. Life will only be fruitful when you go the distance. In addition to that, do not participate in any gambling or speculative activities.

SELF-ELEMENT Metal 2022

Yang and Yin are the outputs and the wealth elements for the Metal Day Masters. As a result, there are likely to be many chances to learn something new and create value from it. It could be a chance to make some money from your talents.

Yang Water is the eating god star for Yang Metal Day Masters. With this, noble people will help you secretly, so use it to your advantage. It will be a good year to learn something new or transform. The only way to understand the opportunities that come your way will be through trial and error. Experiment with the ideas you receive.

For the Yin Metal Day Masters, Yang Water is the hurting officer star. Note that it will be a year of self-reflecting. Take this time to learn more about yourself and improve your body and mind. Do not worry, though, about any hurdles which come your way. Help will be readily available. You shouldn't resist changes or be afraid to take the first step for that alone.

How to succeed in 2022

To thrive in 2022, find ways to gain new perspectives and insights. Pursue all educational chances and capitalize avenues to widen your network or circle. Should you find yourself stuck, talk to those who know better.

ANIMAL RELATIONSHIPS

Chinese New Year is a cultural event that is celebrated around the world. Also known as the Spring Festival, this turning point in time is more than just a cut-off point in the calendar. It also indicates where the annual energy changes have set, and a whole new influence on one's luck would begin. The upcoming year with its many challenges, chances, and changes, would be the year of the Water-Tiger. While the imagery of the 12 animal signs is an integral part of Chinese Astrology, it is literal. Originally, they were merely designations of a particular period; no different from calling a month February, March, and April. However, as what ancient scholars would come to know by observing the influences these blocks of time offer, their findings would establish a form of Chinese Astrology known as Pa Chee, Four Pillars of Destiny, or BaZi. This system can identify opportunities and challenges you may face in the year ahead.

DID YOU KNOW YOU ARE MORE THAN YOUR ANIMAL SIGN?

Almost everyone knows the 12 animal signs in Chinese Astrology – Rat, Ox, Tiger, Rabbit, Dragon, Snake, Horse, Goat, Rooster, Dog, and Pig.

You might also, at some point, proclaim with pride which animal sign you belong to based on the year you were born.

But did you know you also have three other animal signs?

In Bazi / Four Pillars, a person is more than the animal sign of their birth year.

Each month, day, and even hour also have their animal sign and, in turn, are present in your astrology chart. So, these different timescales affect different aspects of your life.

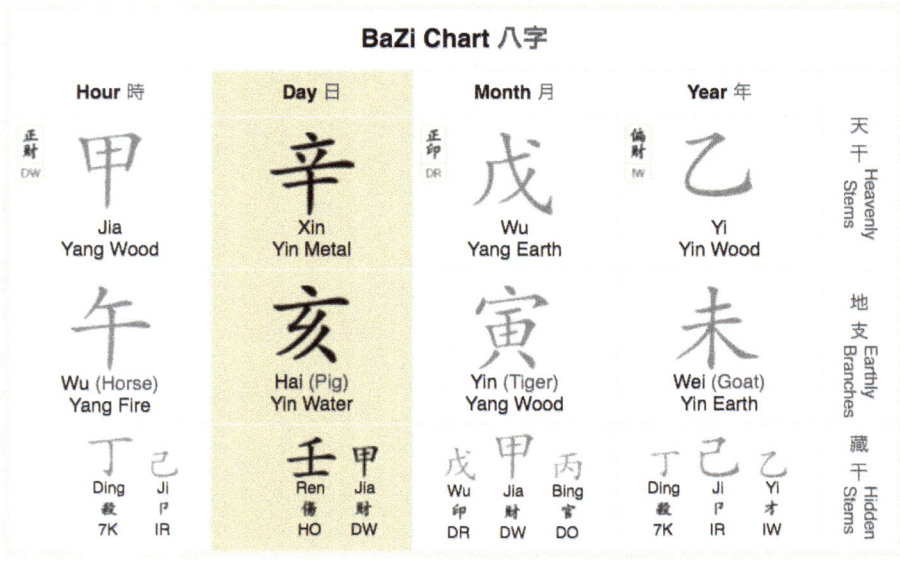

THRIVING AND SURVIVING IN 2022

Depending on where an animal is within the Bazi - Four Pillars of Destiny chart will indicate which area of life it will influence and affect.

- The hour pillar relates to your *assets/investments*, health, ideas, dreams, hope, inspirations, assets. Your contribution, education, and your children,

- The day pillar relates to a *spouse*, personal relationships, views, thoughts, feelings, and home environment.

- The month pillar relates to *career* work performance business outlook. And parents.

- The year pillar relates to *network*, representing your friends, colleagues, social circle, appearance (how you are viewed especially by others), and relationships.

First it is good to know which animal is present in the month you are born.

January is month of Ox

February is month of Tiger

March is month of Rabbit

April is month of Dragon

May is month of Snake

June is month of Horse

July is month of Goat

August is month of Monkey

September is month of Rooster

October is month of Dog

November is month of Pig

December is month of Rat

Secondly if you know your time of birth you can work out which Chinese Animal hour your where born in.

Ox hour is 01.00 – 02.59 am
Tiger hour is 03.00 – 4.59 am
Rabbit hour is 05.00 – 6.59 am
Dragon hour is 07.00 – 8.59 am
Snake hour is 09.00 – 10.59 am
Horse hour is 11.00 – 12.59 am
Goat hour is 01.00 – 02.59 pm
Monkey hour is 03.00 – 4.59 pm
Rooster hour is 05.00 – 6.59 pm
Dog hour is 07.00 – 8.59 pm
Pig hour is 09.00 – 10.59 pm
Rat hour is 11.00 – 12.59 am

Do You have AN Abundance of wealth opportunities in 2022?

The **Snake, Goat, and Monkeys** have wealth-creating opportunities in 2022.

Using the right action, wealth can be created if you are born in a Snake, Goat, or Monkey Year, Month or Hour.

The Strongest opportunity is in the Month and Hour pillars.

If you have Snake, Goat or Monkey in your:

Year steps up your networking, marketing, social media presence for a business, corporate, and career.

Example: Your value will increase but must match action, e.g.,

The month represents change, meaning make changes, acting is pivotable for change.

Hour represents opportunity and risk.

Hour acquires investment share opportunities.

ARE YOU MOST LIKELY TO STEP UP AND SUCCEED in 2022?

The **Rabbit, Snake, Rooster, Monkey, and Pig** are the most likely to succeed as TITIANs in 2022.

If you have Rabbit, Snake, Rooster, Monkey or Pig in your:

Year   Networking opportunities come your way.

Month You can excel in your career or business.

Hour   Activity creates action and success.

2022 POWER OF THE SPOKEN WORD – THE VOICE

The **Tiger and Rabbit** have the power of "Influence," meaning what you say influences the outcome for others. You have the power of dictation, the power of the spoken word to influence others.

Rabbit has the strongest influence and power if found in the luck pillar; what you say, people will follow.

Tiger is "The Boss" in 2022. Whatever the Tiger says, people will follow…

ACADEMIC LEARNING STAR

The **Tiger, Snake, and Dog** have the "**learning star**" easily acquire learning and understand new skills and education. Especially if seen in the Hour pillar.

LEADERSHIP IN 2022

The **Tiger Horse and Rooster** will have leadership and power in 2022.

If born in the **Month** Tiger, Horse or Rooster, you will have leadership and power and will find it easy to advance into positions of power. You will be given opportunities of ultimate power to make decisions. With the right action, results are assured.

But **Tiger** may feel the pressure of making decisions.

The **Horse** activates by showing the way like a general.

The **Rooster** leads by example like an emperor; people will look up to the Rooster for leadership and decisions.

PROSPERITY STAR

The animal most likely to put on weight is **Pig** in 2022 as has **'prosperity star.'**

Put on weight in 2022 but can use for good and build muscle instead.

THRIVING and SURVIVING IN 2022…
YES OR NO TO A NEW JOB!

Do you stay put, or is 2022 the time to find a New Job?

Suppose you are born in a **Snake, Goat, or Rooster** month. DO NOT change jobs in 2022; no need to change as you are about to reap the rewards from your past efforts.

How DO YOU find a new job in 2022?

Review which month you are born in for the best indication of getting the new job or position.

Tiger	Do Internship
Rabbit	Referral ask to be referred
Dragon	Employment agency
Horse	Go direct / official www / go to company's www
Monkey	Self advertising - blow your own horn
Dog	Social media
Rat	Cold call
Ox	Head-hunter to position you
Pig	Networking

POPULARITY STARS OF 2022

The **Horse and Monkey** gains popularity, sudden fame, recognition, and networking opportunities.

If **Horse or Monkey** in:

Year   Fame is derived from a social network, colleagues, and friends.

Month   Career recognition.

Hour   Kids, students, employees, creation, e.g., book, product.

ROBOCOP STAR

The **Horse** in 2022 is married to work and can neglect love, relationships, and family.

If a horse in **Year**, busy with networking and external pursuits.

Great Expectations

Who is likely to Expect a baby in 2022?

The **Tiger, the Horse, and Monkey** have the '**great expectations star.**'

Suppose you have the Tiger, Horse, or Monkey in your hour pillar. Your chance for a baby is high.

If you have the Tiger, Horse, or Monkey in your year, pillar friends around you will give birth.

24 MOUNTAIN STARS CHINESE ASTROLOGY ANIMAL INFLUENCES

People are under the notion that destiny is set in stone. However, that is far from the truth. Like many other things in this world, one can even alter destinies. We make our destinies. The stars that come with our animal signs show us all the advantages and disadvantages, like cues, which may exist throughout the year. How we react and behave upon receiving those cues is how we take our destiny into our own hands.

Understanding the 24 mountains and stars enables you to understand your luck. Having all auspicious stars does not inherently mean that you're going to have a fantastic year, and adversely having all inauspicious stars does not mean you're doomed. All in life is about balance, yin and yang, action and consequence. Merely acting as catalysts, luck isn't so much what you come by, but rather what you make of it. Understanding your stars helps you navigate which turns to take and which roads to avoid.

The **Rat and Pig** benefit from **NEUTRAL** life force energy, meaning extra effort may be required as life force energy is like a resource element and gives you the impetus to do things; when neutral, you will need to push yourself that little bit more to feel motivated.

The **Ox, Tiger, Rabbit, Dragon, Goat, and Dog** benefit from **WEAK** life force energy, usually resulting in low motivation levels and easily discouraged.

The **Snake, Horse, Monkey, and Rooster** all benefit from **STRONG** life force energy, helping with clarity of vision to get the best from the Tiger year. Effectiveness in ideas and actions will bring productive results. Keep goals clear in your mind, and the world is your oyster.

The **Ox, Tiger, Rabbit, Dragon, Goat, Monkey, Rooster, and Dog** have the "**Big Auspicious Star,**" bringing unexpected windfall luck, which equals an edge and prosperity to succeed.

The **Tiger, Rabbit, Dragon, Snake, and Goat** have the "**Small Auspicious Star**," bringing small victories and small windfall luck.

The **Rat, Yang, and Yin Water Day** masters have Wealth and Financial success as "**Water**" represents wealth luck. The Water element in your chart will also represent cash flow.

The **Snake** has "**Heavenly Seal**," enjoying the patronage of powerful mentors, with help coming without you having to seek it.

The **Rabbit and Dog** have the "**Golden Deity**," enjoying celestial fortune, bringing better trust of your instincts.

The **Pig** has the "**Robbery Star**," be mindful not to be taken by conmen or get cheated by others. Robbery Star brings money loss and betrayal.

The **Rat** has the "**Natural Disaster Star**," a star that can put you in harm's way in all manners of natural misfortune, e.g., floods, fire, earthquakes, tsunamis, viruses, and disease. The Rat must carry spiritual protection for 2022: Cross, Ganesha, or Brum pendant.

The **Rat**, **Horse, and Goat** have the "**Yin House Star**," bringing the danger of sickness, virus, disease, and general lack of energy. Protection is necessary.

The **Tiger and Monkey** have the '**Travelling Horse**' present, which means there will be change, movement, and travel. If you have the Tiger in one of your pillars, travel or change could be coming to your business, career, or private life.

The **Pig, Horse, and Dog** are in '**Harmony**.' Therefore, if you have one of these animals in one of your pillars, you can expect a good and harmonious year for your business, career, education, home environment, and personal relationships.

The **Pig** has an extra advantage in 2022 as "**Secret Friend**" to the Tiger, bringing special luck to your chart.

The **Horse and Dog** have special "**Allies**," bringing special luck to your chart.

The **Rooster and Rabbit** have the '**Flower of Romance**' present, which indicates "Peach Blossom" for people born in the year or day of **Rooster or Rabbit**. This means your social life can be quite busy for the year. People will be more attracted to you, and you may make new friends. It also indicates new romance or friendships can be anticipated in your personal and professional life.

Rabbit is "**Peach Blossom**."

To develop a relationship this year, the combination of Tiger seeing Horse Seeing Dog will trigger luck. Two or three animals need to be present: Horse Day, Dog Month, Tiger Year.

Spouse stars pull in for 2022 are **Rat and Ox or Monkey, Rat, Dragon**.

2 or 3 harmonious animals must be present on the day pillar to pull in relationship luck.

The **Rooster** has "**Yi Duo**" this star acts as a magnification star which makes good things better and terrible things worse. It amplifies day-to-day living with extreme highs and devasting lows. This star can bring much colour but also be exhausting and draining.

The **Ox, Goat, Rabbit, and Snake** have '**Noble people luck**.' Nobleman luck is like secret protection; it helps you make everything smooth and positive.

The **Tiger** year is **Nobleman** year for people born in Ying Metal year or Ying Metal Day. These are years ending with 1. Such as 1951, 1961, 1971, 1981, 1991…. etc. Nobleman means an angel is coming from Heaven to provide rescue and support, and such Nobleman often solves troubles by making the year more comfortable and smoother. People who have Nobleman in 2022 can take the chance to make progress and develop new projects.

The **Tiger and Monkey** have the '**Academic star'** this year. There is the chance to excel in studies and learning if you have the Tiger or Monkey as one of your pillars.

Yin Fire in the heavenly stem of year, month, or hour brings extra luck in the form of the "**Heaven Star of Virtue,**" which refers to kindness or charisma. It indicates you have a better chance of success and even the ability to escape from danger. If it is in the hour pillar, it can assist your career. A lot of celebrities and reality television winners have this in their pillars.

The **Ox and Snake** have the '**Loneliness star'** this year. If you have the Ox or Snake in one of your pillars, you may experience periods of solitude or loneliness in your personal and business life.

This year, the Dragon and Dog have the 'Star of Arts,' which refers to having an interest in the arts or an increase in artistic qualities. Therefore, the Dragon or Dog in a pillar indicates more artistic influences in your business and home environments and your relationships. This Star also brings with it a tendency for loneliness.

The **Dragon and Rat** will find themselves overly '**emotionally sensitive'** in 2022. Very important to let go, not to be overly sensitive or emotional; 2022 is not a year to hold grudges.

The **Dragon and Dog are** likely to seek advice from the wrong person, be very careful who you seek advice from.

The **Dragon** also has an ear for confiding; you will find people come to you to confide; tears may be shed. Choose who you give your energy to wisely.

The **Goat and Monkey** are the **big spenders and impulsive buyers** in 2022. Be mindful of big spending and impulsive buying. Be conscious of spending and invest wisely in self, education, investments instead of trivial impulses.

The **Rat** is best not to offend others; karma will come back to bite you. Be mindful you don't betray someone if betrayal in Year will affect your networking. Month your career or business. Day your relationships. Hour staff or children.

The **Rabbit and Horse** are the most likely to experience a new epiphany, make changes, and come to major realization in 2022.

The **Monkey and Snake** are more "**Spiritually inclined**" with the power of Third Eye Opening.

2022 brings spiritual growth, the ability to look inwards, better growth, and understanding.

See truth = third eye

A time to explore own self, life path journey.

You become sensitive and available to detect energy.

The '**Clash animal'** of the Tiger is the **Monkey**.

A clash means conflict and disharmony.

The **Tiger and Monkey** is a clash between Wood and Metal. This clash relates to traffic accidents, especially land-related accidents, as both the Tiger and Monkey are traveling stars.

The clash will occur whenever the two animals appear together simultaneously.

The most unstable months will be February and August 2022, as the Tiger and Monkey represent these months, respectively.

The combination of **Tiger and Monkey** (wood and metal) brings physical accidents and limb damage. Additionally, it will be felt the most in the Tiger hour (3 am – 5 am) and in the Monkey hour (3 pm – 5 pm) of each day.

The clash between the **Tiger and Monkey** is a serious clash between wood and metal elements. Both Tiger and Monkey are traveling stars, so the clash will often bring serious traffic accidents, especially car crashes. Therefore, people born in the years of Monkey must be particularly careful in 2022. As metal and wood clashes, the danger could be associated with cars or machinery. If you have such a clash, you must take extra care when driving cars and traveling. Therefore, for people born in the year of Monkey, it is recommended that they carry the pendant of a Pig which will help repel the Tiger to minimize the negative influence of the clash.

Monkey-born people will experience a turbulent year with more movements, traveling, and changes. It is advised to engage in more movements, such as moving houses or offices. Traveling is also good, but one should refrain from driving fast cars and avoid going straight towards the Northeast direction as it is the direction of the Grand Duke in 2022. Monkey is also advised to minimize activities involving fast-paced sports, such as skiing, car racing, etc.

If you have the **Monkey** in your hour, day, month, or year pillar - it indicates feelings of conflict and disharmony. That may affect your business, career or education, home environment, and health, as well as personal and professional relationships.

This clash is only active and can cause trouble when these two animals are present simultaneously, e.g., year, month, day, or hour, if you are a 'weak' strength of elements.

If you are a 'strong' strength of elements, you can expect reverse effects (good luck) upon you.

Tiger year and day born people will also face challenges due to offending the "Grand Duke." This brings disharmony, irritation, worries, frustration, and sickness. The Grand Duke is an energy point from the Universe classified as a God. It will be favourable for Tiger-born people to carry a Pig amulet /token and keep noise and interaction in the Northeast of homes to a minimum.

The **Tiger** forms a three-penalty relationship with the Snake and the Monkey. Such a penalty is a hidden danger and may cause disharmony, worries, irritations, or hidden sickness. **Monkey or Snake** born people are recommended to carry the pendant of the Pig to minimize such penalty influence in the year of the Tiger.

The **Tiger** is also part of a serious configuration in animal astrology called the "**Three Fire Penalty**." This configuration is formed when the three wood, fire, and metal animals Tiger, Snake, and Monkey appear simultaneously. Such penalties can cause serious misfortunes related to fire elements such as fire disasters, nuclear energy accidents, the eruption of a volcano, even inflammation, skin and breathing organ, or intestine diseases.

ANIMAL INFLUENCES 2022 BRIEF

RAT Wealth, Natural Disaster, Yin House, Neutral LIFE force energy.

OX Big Auspicious, Nobleman, Loneliness, Weak LIFE force energy.

TIGER Big Auspicious, Small Auspicious, Travelling Horse, Academic, Tai Sui, Weak LIFE force energy.

RABBIT Big Auspicious, Small Auspicious, Flower of Romance, Peach Blossom, Nobleman, Golden Deity, Weak LIFE force energy.

DRAGON Big Auspicious, Small Auspicious, Star of Arts, Weak LIFE force energy.

SNAKE Small Auspicious, Nobleman, Heavenly Seal, Loneliness, Strong LIFE force energy.

HORSE Harmony, Allies, Heavenly Seal, Golden Deity, Yin House, Strong LIFE force energy.

GOAT Big Auspicious, Small Auspicious, Yin House, Weak LIFE force energy.

MONKEY Big Auspicious, Travelling Horse, Clash, Academic, Strong LIFE force energy.

ROOSTER Big Auspicious, Flower, Yi Duo, Strong LIFE force energy.

DOG Big Auspicious, Harmony, Allies, Golden Deity, Star of Arts, Weak LIFE force energy.

PIG Harmony, Allies, Travelling Horse, Robbery, Neutral LIFE force energy.

RAT (1924, 1936, 1948, 1960, 1972, 1984, 1996, 2008, 2020)

Enduring, persistent, adaptable, accepting, brave, curious, and forgiving. Rat-born people can talk too freely and can be accused of gossiping. They are fast, determined, will not stay put, and have many changes and moves in all areas of their lives. They are excited by new things.

Winning in 2022, The Rat enjoys winning energies from the flying 1 Victory star this year. This brings you competitive luck, allowing you to emerge triumphant in whatever you choose to pursue. It is a year to control your expenditure while going after what you want and challenging yourself with big goals! However, caution is recommended as you have the natural disaster star and three killings, which generate obstacles out of your control. If you activate your strengths and suppress your afflictions, 2022 has a huge promise for you!

- Wealth luck
- Natural Disaster Star
- Flower of Romance
- Sitting with 3 Killings
- Yin House Star
- Weak life force energy

BEST MONTHS - August, January 2022

BAD MONTHS - March, June

RAT Overall Forecast for The Year

2022 shows neutral life force energy for the Rats, but do not fret. It just means extra effort may be required. There are numerous ways to use your tenacity and stars to your benefit. After all, life is about comprehending that there cannot be a rainbow without a little rain.

With the presence of the yin house star in your year, you may stand chances of accidents and receiving some bodily injuries. For instance, your injuries will probably just be minor surgeries and cuts. Even something as small as a paper cut, perhaps. Nevertheless, it probably will be in your best interest to try and avoid any type of dangerous activities this year.

All are wise to avoid becoming entangled in fights, robberies, or illegal business activities. These activities will more than likely bring about monetary losses and physical injuries. Should you intend to stay in the best of health and safety, stay alert and be smart with the choices you make.

Be mindful of the natural disaster star; this inauspicious star notes the possibility of being in places prone to natural calamities. You could find yourself stuck in typhoon areas, hurricanes, or even a massive flood this year. Rats are apt to be in situations where you're faced with nature's wrath because of the energies of this star. When you are presented with opportunities to increase those chances, take a step back in the opposite direction instead. In addition to that, also make sure always to double-check the weather and be properly insured wherever you go in 2022. You may not go through any of it, but it never hurts to be just a tad more careful.

Wealth

In terms of wealth, you will not exactly hit the jackpot. Only with hard work can you reap great rewards. To put it briefly: no pain, no gain. One way best recommended to help rats with their wealth in 2022 is to get creative in business. Enhance what you're working on and find means to only expand from thereon. Innovative ways can work in your favour.

Career

Taking risks may not be the best way to go about your career. Rats will nevertheless find themselves rather cautious this year. This can bring benefits but being too safe will not help with insight. Instead, try to look and plan. Use your time to engage in training. On top of that, be careful when socializing with others, for you may find yourself offending people. Should that happen, you may be forced out altogether.

Relationships

You may have a flower of romance in your chart, meaning you will be feeling good about yourself. However, your peach blossom luck isn't strong this year. Due to that, you could find yourself pinned down in a rather boring relationship. You might be tied down to a partner who lacks initiative and refuses to engage in social activities. Remember, though, it takes two to tango and makes a relationship work. Meanwhile, for rats who do not have their eyes set on anyone, you could very well be putting all your energy toward your careers.

Health

With neutral life force energy and so much water energy about, the coming year is one you need to tackle with wariness. You have a high possibility of encountering accidents or getting injured. You could very likely hurt yourself, especially physically, so you should be careful in everything you do. With so many traveling stars, you must pay more attention to traffic, for you may be prone to get into accidents.

OX (1925, 1937, 1949, 1961, 1973, 1985, 1997, 2009, 2021)

The hardest worker of all the animals; Ox-born people are persistent, take the pressure off others, have high stamina, and carry heavy burdens. They can be stubborn, reveal little about themselves (including their health), and seldom complain. They also tend to stay put for extended periods.

The Ox looks forward to an extremely satisfying year with success luck firmly on your side. Your home sector plays host to the Current Prosperity 8 Flying Star, indicating that for you, this is a good time to build for the future. The Prosperity Star brings you great wealth, luck, and lucrative opportunities. You also share a Big Auspicious Star with those born under the Tiger sign, suggesting that working with Tigers bodes well for you in 2022. This is a year to strengthen your financial position, so don't let money-making opportunities pass you by. Look for opportunities, get your timing right, and leverage your most auspicious months, including May, December, and January 2022. There is so much good fortune in store for the Ox!

ANNUAL FLYING STAR: Prosperity 8 Flying Star

- Big Auspicious
- Yearly Killings
- Sitting 3 Killings
- Nobleman Luck
- Loneliness
- Weak Life force energy

BEST MONTHS - May, December, January 2023

BAD MONTHS - August, October

OX Overall Forecast for The Year

The year 2022 for Ox comes with a mixed bag of luck. Auspicious and inauspicious stars, requiring merely you to be vigilant in overcoming any challenges 2022 should bring.

The Ox is most favourable for romance, a year for strengthening love and current relationships. Two thousand twenty-two favours romantic tidings, encourages meeting new people, and boosts positive social activities. On a non-romantic plane, it helps attract new customers, clients, or maybe even fans.

Travel is indicated, meaning you will constantly be presented with convenient access to places, people, and an enjoyable lifestyle. However, be extra mindful and stay on your toes whenever you go out.

The Ox is gifted the possibility of engaging with a highly skilled medical practitioner. This can work in your favour if you're ever in need of an effective treatment. But on the flip side, with weak health luck and energy, you could encounter health problems and setbacks. The possibility of falling ill is high for the Ox in 2022. To avoid ill health, try and detox, follow a health regime, and attend routine medical check-ups.

With the appearance of the Loneliness star, the Ox may be affected emotionally. You may feel down and experience emotions of loneliness and unwantedness. Anxiety and agitation could also follow as mental and emotional anguish can take a toll on you if you let it.

With so much happening, a negative impact on your finances is highly probable, so avoid lending money to others or making major investment deals.

Be mindful that the Ox's weak life force energy doesn't cause potential delay, setbacks, and disappointments with so much action in the Tiger year. The best way to handle this is to find an alternative solution to important matters and opt to pivot in a new, smarter direction each time you get the chance to do so.

If you think that luck comes on its own, you are wrong. There isn't anything in this world that would come to you without putting in at least a little effort. An analogy is that effort is the fuel, and luck is the car. Your car could be a million bucks, but without the fuel to move it, it would just be a nice piece of stagnant metal. Likewise, luck can only be activated when you put in the work…

Wealth

2022 shows a steady upward trend in terms of gaining wealth. Wealth luck is positive, as you are rather crafty at maintaining a good balance between the money flowing out and the money coming in. Business appears to be stable, and via efficient social networking with the right people, you easily stand a high chance to procure great profits.

Career

Taking the initiative with everything is a good step; however, now is not the right time to go the extra mile. Instead, stick to cultivating the right working attitude and keeping your feet steady on the ground. Having high aims is crucial, but you have to make sure you can match. Do not aim for the sky when you're incapable of reaching it at present.

Relationships

2022 looks bright. You are likely to meet a suitable partner for those who are single. However, a word of advice: do not be too aggressive or forward when you meet someone you like. It's good to be honest about your feelings, but sometimes a little mystery may help you push all the right buttons.

Health

2022 is the season for illnesses. With weak life force energy, you need to beware. Colds and coughs will be more frequent, maybe because of your immune system. You could also face a lot of psychological tension. One way to get around it is by moving closer to nature. Being surrounded by natural elements of the earth can improve your health and relieve your mood.

TIGER (1926, 1938, 1950, 1962, 1974, 1986, 1998, 2010, 2022)

Sensitive, alert, and with a lot of energy, Tiger-born people are influential and bad-tempered. They usually lead, take chances, and have fortunate lives. They are also independent and very protective of their family.

2022 Tiger is the ruling sign of the year and has the Grand Duke/Tai Sui backing – this can be powerful luck for you. Promising a big year for wealth, the TIGER has much to gain. As the ruling sign of 2022, you enjoy powerful support from the Grand Duke/Tai Sui. The Prosperity 8 Flying Star energizes you and brings the excellent potential for amassing great wealth. Big and small auspicious stars attract the kind of luck that facilitates notable wins and big successes. Set clear goals for yourself, as you are perfectly poised to attain whatever you aim for. Make this a year to remember by surrounding yourself with the right people and taking full advantage of all your lucky stars.

- Small Auspicious
- Big Auspicious
- Tai Sui – supports and helps overcome obstacles
- Travelling Horse
- Academic Star
- Weak Life force energy

BEST MONTHS - May, July, December

BAD MONTHS - August, October

TIGER Overall Forecast for The Year

2022 Tiger has the Academic star bringing the extra advantage to understand complex information. This year will be an opportunity for tigers to learn the how's of things, especially if you're engaged in studies and academic performances. Should tigers choose to work for others this year, they will hone better skill sets abilities to solve disputes, cultivate better management, and exuberate leadership skills. If they choose to work for themselves on a winning streak, they will build better business skills and tools and obtain relevant information and knowledge.

Tigers will also spend the year attracting quite a bit of attention with the presence of the Grand Duke/Tai Sui. It symbolizes the appearance of an emperor having all eyes on him. It will help others connect with you and increase their sense of admiration for you. It is a good start, especially if you have something to offer.

On the other hand, Tigers will also face the Grand Duke star. This star can bring about disruption to your lives. There will be plenty of problems to overcome, and if you dislike change, this year could result in a rather uncomfortable time. Adversely, if you like to change, this may just be the right time for you.

Unfortunately, there could be some negative implications health-wise, particularly mental health issues like stress and depression because your emotional health energy is weak.

2022 may propagate tigers to face petty squabbles and head-butting with family members and loved ones.

Betrayal and backstabbing come with the territory of success, so be wary of who you trust and do not overly depend on anyone, whether that may be at home or the workplace.

Two thousand twenty-two plans may not always fall through but stay level-headed and mind the things you say. Poor planning could set a delay in work-related projects, but the best thing Tigers can do is cope with changes as they present themselves.

Wealth

In terms of wealth, be sure to balance income and expenditure. There isn't an obvious increase in terms of income, so if you're not careful with the money you spend on things, you could face financial difficulties in the short term. It is important to be prepared if a crisis happens.

Career

On the front of your career, you are rather likely to be recognized by your higher-ups due to your stellar performance at the workplace. Nevertheless, there is always room for improvement and growth. Someone new to the job can never learn too much. However, you must be careful of petty people. Keep a low profile and just focus on what is required of you.

Relationships

Your hectic schedule at work will put a dent in your work-life balance. Tigers will find themselves with little to no time for relationships. This can make a promising marriage wither and dry up. It will be an important year for you to navigate the changes that happen in your relationships. The effort you put in is what you will get out. Keep that in mind.

Health

2022 should be the year you stay away from metal and sharp objects. Travel incidents will rise, and your emotional health is fragile. Avoid excessive eating and drinking as it can affect your digestive system. Practice a good health regime; stay away from food that isn't fully cooked and oily if you want to keep your health good.

RABBIT (1915, 1927, 1939, 1951, 1963, 1975, 1987, 1999, 2011)

Exceptionally sensitive, alert, intelligent, and honest. The minds of the Rabbit-born move at great speeds. They are clever, analytical, and will always have backup plans. They are soft, emotional, sensitive, and quick-tempered but rarely expressed. They can be impatient vulnerable, but unbelievably, they are a great asset to have in your life.

2022 Rabbit enjoys romance and relationship luck! Those of you seeking love will find it easily and readily. If you are looking to get married, this is a promising year to do so! The Rabbit also sees the arrival of many helpful people able and willing to help you. Do not turn away overtures from others. Cultivate your inner confidence and listen to mentors. You have excellent robust success and inner confidence! You are blessed with divine energies from the Golden Deity Star, bringing benevolent people and wise mentors your way. Big and Small Auspicious set the stage for life-changing growth, a year when you can make great things happen for you! You need to watch for quarrelsome energies despite enjoying celestial luck as they pose a problem. However, if you employ your innate diplomacy, you have every opportunity for a lucky year.

- Small Auspicious
- Big Auspicious
- Golden Deity
- Flower of Romance
- Peach Blossom Star
- Nobleman Luck
- Weak Life force energy

BEST MONTHS - July, November

BAD MONTHS - March, June, August, December

RABBIT Overall Forecast for The Year

2022 Rabbit has luck from the heavens with the appearance of the Golden Deity. You will find yourself with the ability to hire the right people to work for you. Adding to that, you will also be blessed with the ability to become friends or partners with those who only add to your benefit. Troubles will seem like a thing of the unknown with the help of the people around you, making all stress fall away.

The Nobleman star is another star that attracts mentors and noble people to your life. By indicating helpful people, you will have the right people show up to support you when you need it the most. They will be great at helping you achieve all your heart's desires, so this is the best time to set your plans, goals, and intentions in motion.

With Flower of Romance and Peach Blossom, your career could take off. All the social networking you're doing will help you gain financially and open new doors in your jobs or businesses. Through serving and protecting others, you will gain more than you'll ever know. This is the year you shine bright like the sun in the lives of those closest to you.

The flip side of Flower of Romance and Peach Blossom is that there could be unexpected intimacy and relationships which sprout in your life this year as well. This is good if you're single; however, beware if you are married or in a committed relationship.

Rabbits could also find themselves drowning a tad in loneliness and isolation throughout the year. You could be one with big dreams, but there seems to be a lack of drive to move forward. Unfortunately, there can be no results without action and no action without passion. Try to overcome these emotions and not overly depend on anyone at work as others will often disappoint.

Health-wise, there could be the presence of minor ailments due to weak life force energy and emotions. To stay healthy, exercise and practice a good diet.

Wealth

For Rabbits, wealth this year will be one with ample job opportunities. You will receive handsome profits from a full-time job, and the money will keep flowing in.

Career

Your great attitude and performance at the workplace will work well for you come the new year. You will stand a chance at gaining a promotion or even a job transfer to a higher, much-esteemed position in the industry you work for. The probability of this happening will also increase if your boss or supervisor is a male.

Relationships

For those of you who are single or in the market for a significant other, then 2022 is your year. You could find yourself intertwined with an office romance. Exciting, but at the same time, be sure to keep your mind sharp and do not let any drama bring negative impacts to your work. Besides that, older people may also set you up on a blind date.

Health

On the health front of health, things are not top-notch. You could be faced with physical and psychological health issues. Suffering from minor diseases, coughs, colds, fevers, gastrointestinal diseases, and indigestion are just a few of the problems that could come your way.

DRAGON (1916, 1928, 1940, 1952, 1964, 1976, 1988, 2000, 2012)

Dragon-born people have great power, wisdom, strength, and energy. They can look down on people, but they work hard and accomplish grand goals. They desire a challenge, gain respect easily, and support others. They are dreamers, creatives, optimists, and are steady and firm. Dragons are particularly good in the business world.

The Dragon is full of great potential in 2022. Lucky stars with relationship / academic four flying stars may lack motivation. This is a year when you can go after the big dreams. The Dragon enjoys a bevy of fabulous stars, indicating a year full of potentially big breaks, the kinds that catapult you onto much bigger playing fields! Aim high but do not spread yourself too thin. The feng shui winds bring popularity, mental agility, and immense networking luck. Weak element luck, however, deters you from reaching your full potential. Aim high but channel your energy wisely and avoid spreading yourself too thin. Hold fast amidst setbacks and stay the course as much success is to be reaped. The Dragon has huge potential for improvements with increased networking luck.

- Big Auspicious
- Small Auspicious
- Star of Art
- Weak Life force energy

BEST MONTHS - August, October, December

BAD MONTHS - February, April, January 2023

DRAGON Overall Forecast for The Year

2022 Dragons bring a year of learning with one foot in front of the other: steady and slow progress. As bad as that may sound to the Dragon, remember that the lesser the action, the lesser the problems. Ultimately, a tunnel always starts dark. There is light at the end; you just need to make sure you're determined enough to walk toward it, despite the odds.

2022 is a year the Dragon becomes more prone to getting into accidents. Especially with the elderly in your family, illness and injuries may be around you. This is a year for you to pay more attention to those around you who may need it. Your support could go a long way, so do be sure to do your part with your family.

The tongue, they say, is sharper than a double-edged sword. You may want to take extra caution when you communicate with other people. You never know when someone feels extra sensitive to what you say, so try not to offend people.

2022 will bring about obstacles and difficulties. You may not see eye to eye with those around you, and you could butt heads with many. However, understanding and learning what makes us different is one of the best parts of life, so do your best to be patient.

Women especially will be in dire need of patience. Women will be on the higher end of getting offended, notably those with a vendetta or anger management issues.

Wealth

Things are looking rather well-balanced for dragons in 2022. Many of you may have a healthy amount of savings, so you may want to consider some moves if you're a businessperson. For example, you could transform your business models if you're not exactly satisfied with the volumes. You may also find yourself receiving some unexpected gains from investments this year.

Career

In terms of career, everything is on the right track. You will find job opportunities from companies offering great positions and pay. However, you need to be sure to weigh the advantages and disadvantages before making any moves. Be firm with people and make your goals as clear as day. Remember, confidence is the way you can rule the world.

Relationships

With no peach blossom or flower of romance, Dragons may not be so lucky in love and relationships in 2022. If you're single in the year 2022, your chances of meeting someone new may be slim. If you are married, though, stability is in the cards. Be aware that you may not get the attention you crave from your spouse if they are preoccupied with work or other issues…

Health

With weak life force energy, health and wellbeing need protecting. You may contract an illness that you had previously overcome. This can be scary, but you can overcome it again, provided you regularly eat and rest well when you're feeling tired and incapable. Besides that, you may also want to take in as much water as possible. This year's weather will be tricky, so be alert for any skin diseases.

SNAKE (1917, 1929, 1941, 1953, 1965, 1977, 1989, 2001, 2013)

Snake-born people are sensitive, wise, alert, and enjoy life to the fullest. Goal orientated, persistent, alert, and loyal. Snake-born people are patient but unforgiving. Do not make them your enemy. Snakes tend to acquire knowledge and then move on. They are determined and can be wise.

The SNAKE is one of the LUCKIEST signs in 2022. Snakes' element luck is off the charts, giving you great vitality and the determination to go after whatever your heart desires. You are blessed with very Strong success, luck, plenty of creative energy, and with heaven luck, putting success readily within reach. Academic and educational success sends accolades to young Snakes and benefits those pursuing new knowledge. For singles, peach blossom is strong, bringing good luck in love as wonderful opportunities await you. This will be an extremely satisfying year, so make it a point to harness your incredibly good fortune!

- Small Auspicious
- Heavenly Seal
- Facing 3 Killings
- Travelling Horse
- Loneliness
- Nobleman luck
- Very Strong Life force energy

BEST MONTHS - August, October

BAD MONTHS - February, November

SNAKE Overall Forecast for The Year

The Snake in 2022 is the one sign with the greatest number of lucky stars.

The Snake is one of the four wealthy stars in Chinese Astrology, receiving secret assistance from noble people. This will be an excellent time for you to get some assets. 2022 is an opportunity to expand your career and challenge yourself with more responsibility. This will indirectly increase wealth. On the other hand, if you have already been investing or own a business, this year will be the year when aid is available to increase your gains.

Snakes will also be blessed with female assistance; male or female, be prepared for assistance from strong women in your life. If anything has been holding you back, now is the time to get started without hesitation. In 2022 you have strength, courage, power, and chances to increase wealth. So long as you can push yourself forward and take concrete steps in the right direction, there can be a success.

Nobleman luck also brings a high status in society, with great achievements, may it be in career or academics. You could find yourself being rather intrigued by the mysterious and have good perceptivity. Always one to finish what you start, creativity, innovativeness, and intellect will be your strong suits this year.

On the negative side of things, snakes could be flooded with emotions of loneliness and isolation. Your immune system will not be at its best, and you could be prone to falling sick. The best thing to do would be to watch your lifestyle and eating habits.

The Snake in 2022 may also forget details, dates, information, and the concept of practicing a healthy lifestyle altogether. What you can do to fix it, though, is to write down all that's important. Technology might just save you. An outbreak of arguments over the smallest things could also play out.

Be mindful of your surroundings as there could be gossip and bad blood around you. Your emotions will be easily compromised this year, which may indirectly push you towards unsmart investments. Stay alert, try to avoid it, and attempt to become stronger, for if you cannot handle the stress of it all, you may crumble.

With so much going on, Snakes will face confusion and uncertainties. The promises you have made unto others will now find their way back to you. Some may be angry, so your best move would be to settle all problems as soon as possible.

2022 could be a year of disputes, lawsuits, and legal entanglements. Thanks to the Three Punishments with the Monkey and Tiger, clashes and arguments with family members may arise. The Three Punishments can also affect your health throughout the year. Falling sick easily and having more physical injuries are likely, so try and avoid avenues that allow that to happen. While you are at it, do also stay away from all things criminal.

Wealth

2022 for Snakes does not appear as stable in terms of wealth luck. They will be prone to suffering some monetary losses throughout the year. Due to that, their best bet would be to adopt conservative strategies when it comes to investments. Prudent financial management is much more suited as compared to other methods. To increase additional income, they can also run a small business.

Career

With a career, you will find yourself traveling quite a bit for internal transfers or business trips. If you're interested in switching jobs or having a career change, best know that this is not the year for it. Instead, work well with the colleagues you do have, especially female supervisors/subordinates. It is favourable. Nevertheless, always maintain your manners to avoid triggering scandals and disputes.

Relationships

Male snakes will have the opportunity to meet someone who shares the same views, life outlooks, and personality traits as themselves. This golden opportunity will be your chance to confess your feelings for them. Don't let them slip away from you. Females, on the other hand, stand lesser chances of romance. This is likely because of unhealed wounds from pasts relationships.

Health

Physically, those with a weak digestive system will need to be careful of what they consume. Exercise control and don't be excessive. Besides that, you could also fall sick or encounter an accident this year, so try and be extra careful. Internally, emotional problems are bound to surface. This could aggravate your moodiness, anxiety, and anxiety as well.

HORSE (1918, 1930, 1942, 1954, 1966, 1978, 1990, 2002. 2014)

Devoted and having inner strength, Horse-born people are persistent, diligent, and determined. They are dependable, honest, loyal, and excited by the challenge. They are proud and independent but need companions. Horses also like comforts, can be frivolous, and love to gossip.

This is a year for the Horse to lay big plans. The Horse is extremely strong in 2022, enabling you to rise above any challenge. Many challenges may come your way; stay focused to achieve your goals. Cosmic winds send you the Star of Future Prosperity, enhancing wealth luck and attracting opportunities to reap long-term success. With strong completion, you have the strength and resilience to make bold strides in whatever direction you choose, so don't let these auspicious energies go to waste! To maximize good fortune, act.

- Harmony
- Allies
- Heavenly Seal
- Golden Deity
- Yin House

BEST MONTHS - June, October.

BAD MONTHS - March, September, December

HORSE Overall Forecast for The Year

The year 2022 for Horses comes with auspicious stars, only a few challenges to gallop over within the year, activating the good ahead that lies in your hands.

You expect some wealth and financial gains throughout the year in terms of money. A rise in pay or an increase in profits and riches could be likened to you receiving a box of gold. You will be rewarded handsomely so that this year would be a great year to uptake a new job with new responsibilities.

This year, your career will also be looking rather well, with business expansions, profits, career success, and work advancement. A promotion and a rise in the ranks may be on the horizon.

Besides financially, this year will bring about fame, vitality, and energy. You are to find yourself more motivated and energized in everything you do. On top of that, your work ethic and efficiency will be noticed by many, indirectly increasing your reputation as well as credibility with others.

The Horse has strong leadership in 2022, helping horses gain credibility and power. You will be beneficial should you accept leadership roles and manage teams. You will be surrounded by good, kind, and sincere people who will offer you strength and assistance if you ever find yourself in need of it.

Horses in 2022 need to be astute as 2022 foresees some problems with documentation, so you should be wary of unfulfilled promises you've made.

You may feel more anxious and impatient than you'd like to be due to emotional volatility and instability. It could end up making you suspicious of your significant other.

Health-wise, 2022 increases your chances of getting into accidents, meeting casualties, and financial losses. These financial losses could also cause legal disputes, legal entanglements, bankruptcy, and unwanted chaos.

Wealth

For Horses in 2022, luck looks well. Morale is high, and things will go as you wish. You may implement plans to expand your business this year, for the outcome seems rather favourable. On top of that, you will have the opportunity to receive a windfall, and with a clear mind, you could very much benefit handsomely from the stock market.

Career

You will find yourself improving rapidly and flourishing within your industry with your job. Your persuasion and leadership skills will be evident at the workplace, and your efforts will not go unnoticed by your superiors. The new setting will need some getting used to, but it won't be something you can't handle. The faster you settle in, the better for you.

Relationships

Love luck is on the average side. You are likely to receive some complaints and dissatisfactions from your lover this year. This may be because you're too focused on work and do not have the time to oversee love matters with your significant other. Emotional conflicts could eventually arise, and you may fall into a situation with no end.

Health

Health condition is good in 2022, and severe diseases will not attack you. So, physically one could say you'd be as healthy as a horse. Unfortunately, the same cannot be said for you emotionally and spiritually. You could have insomnia, an endocrine disorder, and a severe hair loss problem throughout the year. Fortunately, with the right effort, you will surpass all hurdles.

GOAT (1919, 1931, 1943, 1955, 1967, 1979, 1991, 2003, 2015)

Stable and determined, Goat-people are hardworking and willing. They are survivors, not leaders, but make effective team members. They are observant, great listeners, and need people around them. Goats like harmony, but they do not like to be alone.

The Goat enjoys excellent success, luck, and glorious energies from big and small auspicious stars! Your inherent charm serves you well, efforts become extra meaningful, and goals become much easier to attain. Be careful not to push too hard; the Illness Star warns you to take care of your health. Put some focus on nurturing relationships, as they will play a big part in how your year turns out. Set yourself up for a splendid year by collaborating with the right animal signs and surrounding yourself with the right people. The Goat's popularity gets you far but watches for the illness star.

- Big Auspicious
- Small Auspicious
- Facing 3 Killings
- Yin House
- Weak Life force energy
- Excellent success luck

BEST MONTHS - June, July

BAD MONTHS - November, January 2023

GOAT Overall Forecast for The Year

Goats begin with happiness. It's a good year to try and look for someone special to build a long-term relationship with. You can strengthen your companionship for those in a committed relationship or married. Advice to achieving happiness: do things that make you happy.

With your career, you could be granted the chance to get a promotion. Your efforts will bear fruit this year, which could increase your authority at the workplace. Superiors will notice you, and a rise in rank will rise in income. However, remember that with great power comes great responsibility.

Goats will also have a way with problems in 2022. From the new relationships and help and support, you will be able to solve big problems, diminishing them altogether (especially customer and employee-employer issues). This will indirectly reduce the impacts you could face from those problems. On top of that, you will also solve problems from 2021.

You will find yourself moving around far and wide for business and studies. There could even be the possibility of changing jobs.

Beware though Goats could also face cash outflow from recklessness. Financial losses due to cheating, swindling, or extravagant spending, especially frivolous things, should be considered.

You will need to pay more attention to elderly relatives, especially senior males, because they may need health support on the plane of health. Take care of your health, particularly common illnesses related to the throat, respiratory system, and large intestine.

Wealth

For Goats, 2022 will be your chance to double your income, especially in attaining a good full-time job. All you will need to do is some good old networking, which will lead to increased performance in sales. Besides that, it will also help you gain the support you need from loyal customers. To steer clear of any financial hiccups, continue to manage your finances wisely.

Career

Like any working adult, you will face difficulties at the workplace. The good news? You will have people willing to get you out of any stump you may find yourself entangled in. However, there will always be villains waiting on the sidelines to take you down, especially when things are going well. Keep a low profile, and just focus on yourself. Besides that, this year also wouldn't be a suitable time for you to switch jobs. Stay where you are, for there could be a big surprise if you're patient.

Relationships

In terms of relationships, things are looking bright! There is relationship progress with those who have partners. You may be enjoying sweet moments with your lover. For those who are engaged, you may want to consider tying the knot in 2022. Though, best beware for married couples, as there are romantic traps around that could threaten your marriage.

Health

On the branch of health, it is an overall positive outlook. As you live healthily, there will be lesser chances for you to be troubled by any severe diseases. Those who have been sick for a long time now may find themselves recovering completely if they are taken care of and rest enough. Nevertheless, do pay attention to any health issues related to the heart or the blood vessels.

MONKEY (1920, 1932, 1944, 1956, 1968, 1980, 1992, 2004, 2016)

Fast thinkers and very adaptive learners, Monkey-born people are creative but insensitive. They do not bear grudges, are highly independent, and make friends quickly. They are helpful, self-confident, high achievers, ambitious, competitive, and rarely give up.

A promising year for the Monkey to catch its big breaks. The Monkey receives TWO Big Auspicious Stars bringing multiple life-changing opportunities! Your superior Element Luck gives you the tenacity to go the distance, so don't just wait for things to fall into your lap. Be clear with your goals, and then go after them! You have the Illness Star to contend with, so take care of your health. However, if you leverage your best months and remedy your afflictions, the year promises great things for the Monkey!

- 2 Big Auspicious
- Travelling Horse
- Academic Star
- Clash animal
- Strong Life force energy

BEST MONTHS - August, October

BAD MONTHS – February, November

MONKEY Overall Forecast for The Year

Due to your career educational goals, monkeys may find yourself traveling more in 2022. There are high chances to cross borders or even go to a different state. The Monkey can also make money online, from international businesses, out of the country, or from a different industry. A great time for expansion, growth, and starting a new business.

Lucky Monkeys can become famous overnight. Try doing something on YouTube or other social media platforms. The attention attained could set off popularity.

Monkeys will also become rather skilled at solving problems. It could be financial, relational, health (finding a doctor/medication), etc. Your ability to do so will help reduce half your problems and produce an overall positive outcome.

Your problem-solving skills will further be strengthened, turning negatives into positives; help from Noble people will come to you when you need it. This is a good star to have for property investments and good deals. It attracts good land into one's life.

The yearly Academic star will help you pass examinations. The group of you will learn and master new knowledge rather quickly. Your excellent academic performances and outstanding literary talents will shine through more immensely. You stand a chance to discover new things with research, so this is a particularly lucky year for scholars and professors.

Unfortunately, the year will also be filled with unsettling and unexpected changes. You will find yourself spending money and losing money. To be smart, best invest rather than blow it off.

With the clash, you may face some challenges throughout the year, but fret not, for all you must do is work a tad bit harder to achieve your goals.

Health-wise, Monkeys will find themselves prone to accidents and injuries, especially during a workout or physical activities. Injuries also include those from water-related accidents.

Wealth

Come 2022; Monkeys may find a slight difficulty in gaining wealth. You could be faced with great monetary losses, so getting involved in high-risk investments or speculative activities would not be your wisest move to make right now. However, you could opt to earn some foreign money. Those involved in business could try their hand at investing in overseas markets.

Career

On the career front, now would be the right time to grab any opportunity which comes for business travel. Show your talents to your leaders, and you will be recognized for your efforts. This may attract you toward a promotion or a salary increase in one way or another. If you are a business entrepreneur, you will certainly be on the right track this year.

Relationships

You could face some unprecedented challenges like a cross-cultural relationship where love is concerned. Sharing a different culture from someone personally may sound easy but is rather difficult. It will come with its own set of challenges. You will be prone to deal with conflicts and maybe even an emotional betrayal in your relationship.

Health

Health this year for Monkeys will not be at its best. There are possibilities to encounter car accidents, so be careful when driving. Women are at risk of having endocrine disorders. On top of that, you will also be plagued with some emotional issues and might have trouble falling asleep at night and getting some much-needed rest.

ROOSTER (1921, 1933, 1945, 1957, 1969, 1981, 1993, 2005, 2017)

Rooster-born people are musical, creative, artistic, imaginative, and inventive. They can be drama queens or kings. They can be focused, and when it is something, they want, they will love it with a passion. They are persistent, know what they want, are great talkers, and are solid negotiators. They are straightforward, honest with others, and they make great friends. Unfortunately, they are sensitive and tend to bottle up their feelings. They will rarely fight back, but it is with full power when they do.

The Rooster enjoys a year of incredible opportunities, feeling wonderfully energized in 2022. Element Luck gives you the energy and impetus to achieve great milestones! Cosmic winds send a double dose of Big Auspicious, bringing all kinds of opportunities worthy of grand celebrations. An opportune year to spread your wings and soar! However, be mindful of money loss and betrayals. Keep your wits about you, for the year holds great success luck for the Rooster-born.

- 2 Big Auspicious
- Flower Romance
- Yi Duo
- Strong Life Force
- Strong Success Luck.

BEST MONTHS - April, June, November, January 2023

BAD MONTHS - March, July, September

ROOSTER Overall Forecast for The Year

A good year with good omens and positivity. In 2022, the Roosters makes unexpected situations favourable. There might be a whole world of problems in-store, but The Rooster solving them will be a breeze.

Those in this animal sign are lucky this year, for they hold the most auspicious luck in 2022: the presence of noble people, bringing happiness and achievements in strong relationships. The Rooster will be thoroughly guided throughout the year, and there will be plenty of opportunities, benefits, and responsibilities that come your way. Assuming a leadership role would be very beneficial in 2022. The Rooster has the following and support of a whole army of people ready to assist and help you, so do not be afraid. You risk loneliness if you fail to marshal the helpful energy of others and instead suffer in silence.

Good food and clothes are the material aspects Roosters will be blessed with. You wouldn't need to worry about money, for the luck of receiving is on your side.

Roosters risk several broken things in 2022. This could involve everything from communication, status, reputation, or material. Possibly a broken car, fridge, air-conditioner, a leaky roof, car problems, phone problems, etc. There will be a lot of minor hassles, but it will not be as big a deal as it sounds.

However, you should also beware of crimes like theft and robberies at home. You could lose important personal items, especially when leaving to travel.

Wealth

Wealth luck looks stellar for Roosters in 2022, especially for those working in industries related to sales, real estate, or the law. There is increased development in the opportunities you offer and multiple sources of clients. However, just because you're making good money doesn't mean you need to go overspending it. Avoid splurging and make hay while the sun still shines.

Career

There is room for career development, no matter the industry you're engaging in. There is never a wrong place and time to grow. Due to this, do not be afraid should you want to make a career shift. It is a suitable time to change right now, so best use it. However, be well-prepared if you decide to leave the company you're at. Complete all handover tasks before resigning to avoid any official or personal disputes with others.

Relationships

All relationships, in general, can get boring if you are passive. Do your best to find the zest in life and reflect that into your relationship with your significant other. For those who have strong desires to meet someone, pay close attention to those around you, especially in the office. Watch out for those of you who are married, as a cold war with your partner may be on the brink.

Health

Where health is concerned, Roosters have high chances of unexpected disasters or undiagnosed disorders happening to them this year. They will face the many risks of undergoing surgery and even suffering from face damage. Beware of the weather and eating habits to avoid these, especially if you are traveling for work.

DOG (1922, 1934, 1946, 1958, 1970, 1982, 1994, 2006, 2018)

Ready for action, Dog-born people gain respect easily, are brave, and take risks. They are helpful, loyal, dependable, determined, competent, and confident. Dogs will not let go of ideas or ambitions and will likely see things through to the end. They are caring and great listeners. They are very efficient and make great workers, but they are not leaders.

The Dog has the benefit of Heaven's Blessings in 2022. The Dog enjoys good stars in 2022, the Heaven Flying Star 6 and the Golden Deity Star, bringing windfalls and a steady stream of helpful people. Big Auspicious benefits those wanting to make big improvements in your life and can bring the big breaks you are looking for! You need to remedy your weak element luck to make the most of the year. The Dog is the most dependable of all the 12 signs, but you must learn to be comfortable being on the receiving end this year.

- Big Auspicious
- Harmony
- Allies
- Golden Deity
- Star of Arts
- Weak Life force energy

BEST MONTHS - March, May, December

BAD MONTHS - April, June, January 2023

DOG Overall Forecast for The Year

For Dogs, 2022 will bring a mixed bag; with the right guidance and effort, any year can work in your favor. You've just got to forget everything that may stop you and focus on the facets which will help propel you.

With the Star of Arts, an artistic star for dogs will help you produce tons of creative things stemming from your inspirations. This may come off as strange and eccentric if you're not creative. But tap into it anyways, for it can only bring about more confidence and independence. There will also be opportunities for career advancement and pursuits toward your professional interests. Certainly, it is a good star to have if you're in sales and marketing.

Adversely though, you may want to be extra careful when it comes to safety in 2022. There could be bleeding, bodily injuries, or harm from accidents. Be sure to avoid putting yourself in situations that could activate that.

2022 brings an increased risk of financial loss and damage to the reputation this year. You might feel compelled to be rather reckless as well as impatient. This will cost you if you're not careful.

Another aspect to look out for in 2022 will be how dogs communicate throughout the year. There is likely miscommunication, so be alert when speaking to others to avoid this.

Wealth

In 2022, Dogs will be granted the chance to attain a large income. This could stem from some creative works. For businesspeople and entrepreneurs, be on the lookout for monetary losses. Your aggressiveness may just cost you. Expenses throughout the year may also be huge, especially in terms of medical fees, so try not to spend money on anything less than needed.

Career

This is the right place to be this year for anyone engaged in the creative industry. Designing, literature, or arts will be prosperous. It will be a sign of appreciation to fall onto loneliness and self-expression. This will probably not be such a great year for those in fields related to eloquence, for instance, consultants and lawyers. Those in business will have trouble finding satisfactory partners and come across those who have no intention to cooperate with others.

Relationships

On the front of love, those who are single will be less active in finding true love. Besides that, if you are in a relationship, you may find more emotional entanglements than you'd like. Peach Blossom Luck isn't too good for dogs in 2022. You are unable to communicate effectively or nicely with others.

Health

Your body will be rather sensitive throughout the year about health. You could easily injure yourself or cause bleeding. You will be especially vulnerable to animal attacks and may get hurt in the following months. Your mental health will not be at its best, and you could find yourself plagued with psychological issues. Whenever you feel down in the dumps, try and avoid consuming alcohol and then driving afterward.

PIG (1923, 1935, 1947, 1959, 1971, 1983 1995, 2007, 2019)

Pig-born people are not in a hurry, sluggish, and not ambitious. They are not very intellectually competitive and have natural humility. They accommodate, are accepting, intelligent, wise, and independent. They can be determined and reliable, and wise in times of crisis.

The Pig enjoys great success luck in 2022. Mentors and helpful people surround you while receiving divine blessings and assistance from the Heaven 6 Flying Star! This brings exceptional mentor luck, benevolent people, and divine assistance whenever you need it. With your secret friend, the Tiger, ruling the year, you can be assured of strong support from all quarters. Element ratings shore up excellent success potential, so set yourself up with ambitious goals. The year brings some afflictions, but these are easily managed. Make this a year to succeed, trust your intuition, and tap into your most auspicious months.

- Harmony
- Allies
- Travelling Horse
- Robbery
- Neutral Life force energy
- Strong success potential

BEST MONTHS - March, October, December

BAD MONTHS - June, August, January 2023

PIG Overall Forecast for The Year

Pigs of 2022 will be blessed; overcoming hurdles and embracing benefits is how 2022 will guide Pigs to a memorable year ahead.

The year will begin by bringing professional progress. You will find yourself blessed with many opportunities for a promotion at the workplace or even a salary increment. The office will be a good environment to be in throughout the year.

We were gifted with prosperity, plenty of happiness, an enjoyable period, a party even, and the means to explore the world. 2022 is a good time for creating lasting memories for loved ones.

You will also be able to remove all obstacles which present themselves in your path, with assistance from friends, family, and colleagues.

On the side of wealth, the Pig can bring in handsome profits. Whether full-time jobs, side-gigs, or businesses, prosperous incomes will grace Pigs throughout the entire year. Besides that, returns on investments will also be satisfying and stable. Fear not, for you will gain the help of the Noble people and will not be alone.

Love and support will be readily available, which will allow Pigs to connect with those of authority and power. A license or permit will be especially good to have when you need approval. Should you be interested in forming partnerships with those in power, it will be time to do it this year.

On the other hand, the challenges begin with indications of disputes, slander, and arguments that may be circling you. This could put a dent in your relationships, so beware.

Pigs may also have negative influences that lead you astray in 2022. The Robbery Star could risk your reputation, especially if you're a business owner, so best keep your eyes on your accounts and the numbers. Be alert to how cash-based things may go missing throughout the year—for instance, belongings, passports, and money. Dangerous sports should be avoided if possible.

Interpersonal relationships do not look too good this year. Meaning an unfavourable time for marriages, as quarrelling, fighting, and resentment may arise. The best advice for Pigs in 2022 would be to avoid self-centred tendencies when dealing with other people.

Wealth

Pigs should learn how to manage their financial accounts to reduce the risk of encountering any sort of fraud or scams in 2022. Any credit issues by customers may lead you down a path of financial crises, so do be careful. Low-risk investment projects seem to have good returns and are rather favourable this year. You may want to try your hand there.

Career

With regards to your career, things are looking rather swell. There is a chance for career advancement, and you may be lifted to another level rather rapidly. You will get good guidance from those willing to help you, especially with a new job position. This will come in handy and aid you in avoiding any detours. What you can do is spend some time maintaining a wide network at the workplace and, at the same time, avoid naysayers.

Relationships

In 2022, you will have great chances of meeting the person you like. If you can actively grasp the opportunity with that person, you will be expected to see quite a satisfying result by the end of the year. However, the same can't be said for those who are married. You stand the possibility of dealing with marital issues. When faced with problems, best put yourself in one's shoes when communicating.

Health

You could find yourself paying a rather hefty price in terms of health if you end up eating or drinking without control. The risk of getting diabetes or hypertension is on a larger scale, and there could be many who may also suffer from obesity. Try your best to practice moderation. Do not be addicted to alcohol and if you have a habit of drinking and smoking, do your best to quit.

ANNUAL FLYING STAR FORECAST FOR 2022

WHAT IS FENG SHUI...

Feng Shui is an objective-driven science. It's about harnessing the energy of your living environment to help you achieve your goals. It's about paying attention to your Mind, Body and the impact of your Surroundings.

Feng Shui at its core is about answering the following question:

Is your environment aligned with your life goals and vision or is it setting you up for failure?

Feng Shui is not simply about just enhancing 'good luck'. Correctly used Feng Shui can help you discover how to tap into the positive vibrational energy of your environment to create meaningful results in your life.

The benefits of working from home

In the past 2 years, many have been working from home or remotely. Though it has become the new norm, initially it posed a few challenges. The distractions coming from those at home, problems arose when communicating with co-workers and clients especially those in sales and marketing. With so many potential setbacks, how do you maintain composure, stay productive, and thrive despite the challenges?

Recent studies have supported the idea that working from home can increase productivity and decrease stress. Research also suggests companies that encourage and support a work-from-home protocol saves money in the long run.

Since one is limited to the confines of working at home, it's best to make it as comfortable as you can. As Feng Shui is about the opportunities and finding the best area in your home to work in, this lets you capitalise effectively on the good energy of a certain area to improve your wealth, network with the right people, or to gain recognition for your hard work.

Use Feng Shui to align the energies in your home or workspace with the energy within you and create the desired outcome or results desired.

Flying Star Feng Shui is one discipline in Feng Shui and Chinese Astrology which incorporates the principles of the five elements, eight trigrams, Lo Shu numbers, and 24 Mountains to analyse the rise and fall of energy in an environment at a particular time. It is one of the most effective Feng Shui practices that bring consequences and fast results. The principle of Flying Star Feng Shui is that each number (Star) in the Lo Shu square, has specific qualities which will bring good or bad luck. The auspicious Stars bring wealth and wellbeing, so areas with these positive Stars should be used for main areas such as living rooms or bedrooms, whilst the inauspicious areas should be used for less frequented areas such as storage rooms or laundries or treated with the appropriate cures.

AUSPICIOUS STARS

1   Lucky Star (Water element)
    Helps attain victory over competition, enhances career promotion and monetary growth.

4   Romance Star (Wood element)
    Good Star which improves romantic opportunities and study and literary fortune for writers and scholars.

6   Power Star (Metal element)
    Associated with good fortune and help from Heaven, brings speculative luck as well as power and authority.

8   Wealth (Earth element)
    Signifies wealth, prosperity, success and happiness, and is regarded as the most auspicious Star of all the nine numbers until 2024.

AFFLICTION STARS

2   Sickness Star (Earth element)
    The illness bringing Star has negative influences on health issues, bringing physical ailments and diseases.

3   Dispute Star (Wood element)
    A bad Star which signifies lawsuits, hostility and quarrels. Brings misunderstandings amongst families, friends and colleagues, trouble with the authorities.

5   Misfortune Star (Earth element)
    Also known as Wu Wang or Five Yellow Star, it is considered the most malevolent and dangerous of the nine Stars; it brings all kind of misfortunes, accidents, losses and death,

7   Violent Star (Metal element)
    This unlucky Star brings loss, robbery and violence to the afflicted sector.

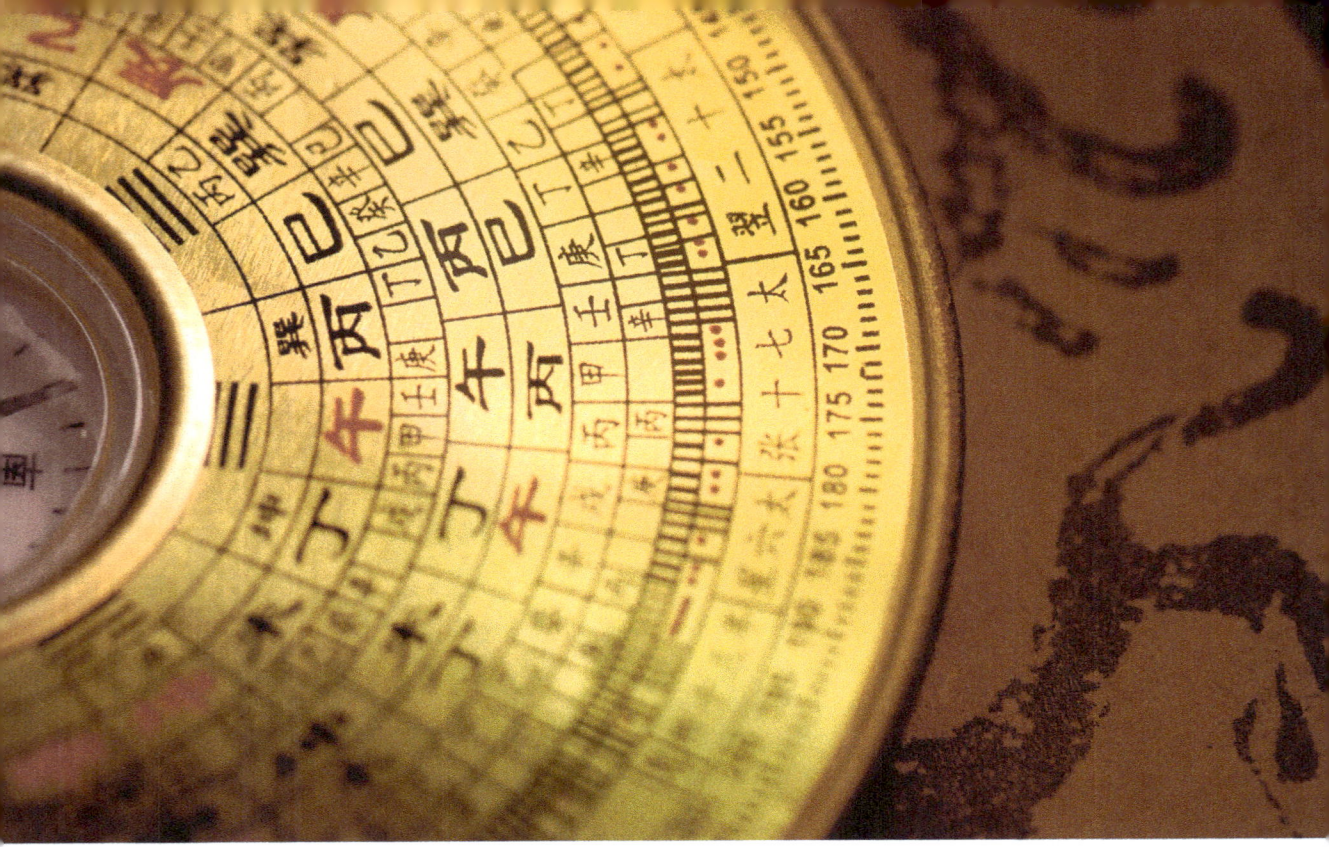

FENG SHUI 2022 FLYING STAR

Getting your Flying Stars right for the coming year and energizing the auspicious sectors of 2022 will ensure you have a successful and smooth-sailing year ahead.

As we move from one year to the next, energy changes, transforming from Yin to Yang, from element to element, from one animal sign to the next. Depending on the ruling element and animal, from one month to the next, the energy in the home and its occupants' changes. Time exerts a very strong impact on your Feng Shui, your luck and destiny.

Good Feng Shui cannot and does not last forever. It must be recharged with small but significant changes every year. Energy must be refreshed, reorganised and re-energized. Spaces and places need rejuvenating. Energy must be kept moving.

The Flying Star formula of Feng Shui is a technical approach that directly addresses the effect of time on the energy of homes and businesses and holds a wonderful promise which enables you to improve your luck tremendously. The 2022 Feng Shui chart maps out the distribution of energy in each of the nine sectors.

We will comprehensively analyse each of the nine sectors of the compass and I will explain how the luck pattern for 2022 will affect your home and office. You will learn to identify which rooms of your home or office will enjoy good luck during the year and which rooms will have negative energy as well. You will learn how to activate lucky sectors and control and suppress sectors that are afflicted this year to protect yourself against misfortune and bad luck.

The best strategy is always to take care of the negative Stars first, and then concentrate on boosting the good Stars. Pay closer attention to the sectors where your main door, living room and bedrooms are located. The luck present in the main door and living room sector affects everyone in the household while the bedroom alters the luck of those who sleep in it. If a bad Star flies into your main door or living room, besides placing a cure here, everyone in the house should also always wear or carry a personal amulet along with them for added protection as this Star affects everyone.

In 2022, the ruling number is 5 and the Lo Shu chart for the year has 5 in the centre. The five in the centre is itself 5 Misfortune Star (Earth element) Also known as Wu Wang or Five Yellow Star, it is considered the most malevolent and dangerous of the nine Stars; it brings all kind of misfortunes, accidents, losses and death.

But the 5 does have a flip side with its essence free feeling: self-emancipating; active; physical; impulsive; energetic; adventurous; resourceful; well-travelled; curious; excitement; change.

Environment with a 5 vibration is vibrant, alive and ever changing. But the challenging aspects of a 5, may sometimes feel living that life is a whirlwind.

COMPASS READING

How to care for your compass

Most compasses are quite sturdy, however, there are some things to be mindful of:

- Never put it near a magnet, this can damage the compass and render it useless
- Do not shake it, as that may dislodge the needle from its pin
- Use a case or the bag that has been provided to protect your compass.

The DON'Ts of taking a compass reading

There are many things that can alter a compass reading, which may result in getting an incorrect reading:

- Do not take a compass reading near a motor vehicle of any kind
- Do not take a compass reading near anything metal; be mindful of belt buckles, mobile phones, metal pens in your hand or pockets as these will alter a reading
- Do not take a compass reading near anything electrical, especially power poles
- Do not take a compass reading standing on pebbles, pea gravel, iron ore or marble.

The DO's of taking a compass reading

To take your reading for Eight Mansions or Bagua*:

1. Stand just outside of your home or business, in front of the building and face the building
2. Lay your compass flat in one hand
3. Have the long part of the (base) section pointing away from you and the compass section closest to you
4. Make sure that the compass is straight
5. Wait for the needle to settle
6. Turn the cover until the point of the needle is right in between the two lines (North)
7. Your compass reading (in degrees) is where the middle line that runs under the compass is pointing into the degrees (black print within the circle of the compass) closest to you.

*You will need this information for working out the Flying Star direction of your home or building for Flying Star and Bagua School of Feng Shui.

Step 1

YOUR Feng Shui and Flying Star house plan and compass reading. Stand in front of your home and look to the road to find the compass facing direction of your home.

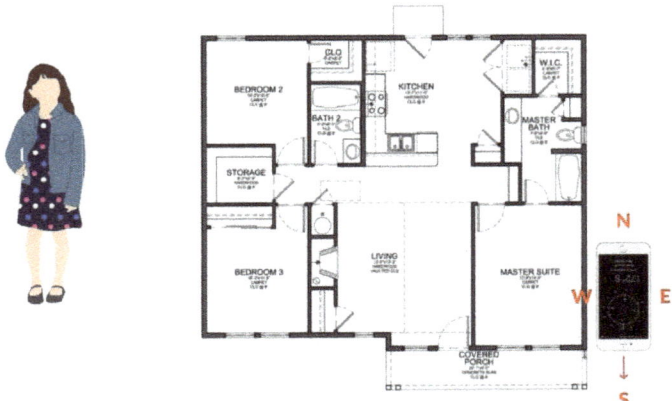

Step 2

Once you know your compass direction, you can superimpose annual flying stars over your plan.

Example of 2022 annual flying stars onto a house plan.

Below is South facing chart example for 2022.

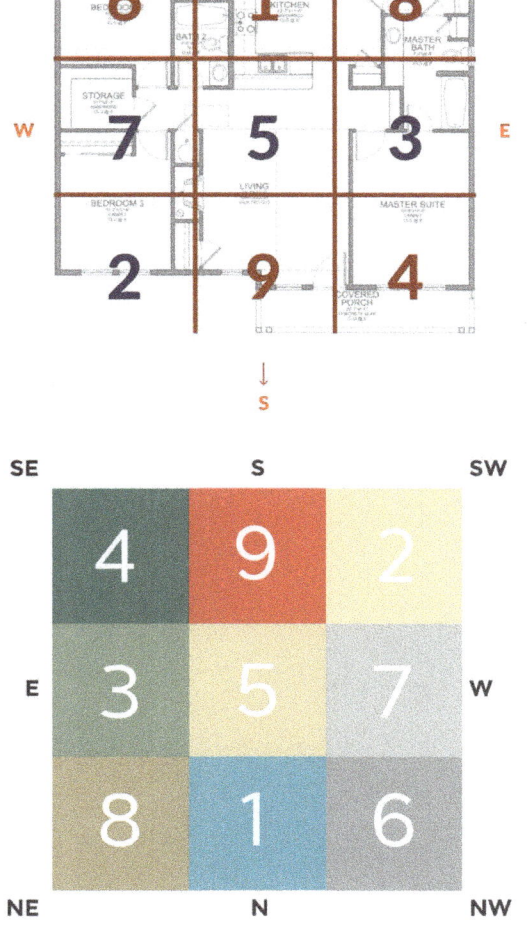

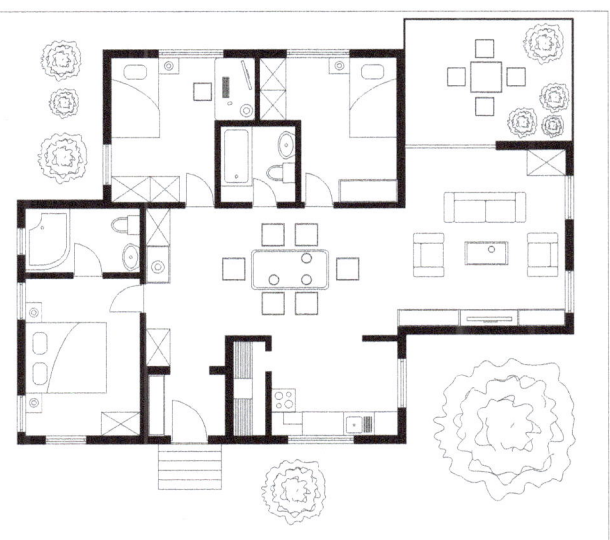

THE MEANING BEHIND THE FLYING STARS

Different types of energy are categorised and identified as the 9 Flying Stars. Though there are many ways these stars could be applied, the most meaningful and practical application of it is its use annually.

Each year, these stars "fly" into different sectors. As their nature is dynamic, a sector in a building could exert positive influence in a year and give off a negative vibe the next year or vice versa. Having awareness of the Flying Stars' configuration is the key to tap into their energy.

The 9 Flying Stars each have their uses and side-effects. Traditionally, they are understood as "auspicious" and "inauspicious", inherently their individual quality is neutral. It is when they are paired with the right intent and the right action that their positive effects can shine.

AUSPICIOUS STARS

North 1 Victory Triumph and Success Star (Water Element): Helps attain victory over competition, enhances career promotion and monetary growth.

Southeast 4 Romance and Literacy Star (Wood Element): Good Star which improves relationship opportunities, study, and literary fortune for writers and scholars.

Northwest 6 Heavenly Luck Star (Metal Element): Associated with good fortune and help from heaven, brings speculative luck as well as power and authority.

Northeast 8 Current Prosperity Star (Earth Element): Signifies wealth, prosperity, success, and happiness; regarded as the most auspicious Star of all the nine numbers until 2024...

South 9 Multiplying Future Prosperity Star (Fire Element): Signifies future prosperity; spurs celebrations, festivities, gatherings, and excellent good luck.

UNFAVOURABLE STARS

Southwest 2 Sickness Star (Earth Element): This illness bringing Star has negative influences on health issues, bringing physical ailments, and diseases...

East 3 Hostile, Conflict and Dispute Star (Wood Element): A bad Star which signifies lawsuits, hostility, and quarrels. Brings misunderstandings amongst staff, clients, colleagues, and trouble with the authorities.

Centre 5 Misfortune and Obstacles Star (Earth Element) also known as Wu Wang or 5 Yellow Star: It is considered the most malevolent and dangerous of the nine Stars. It brings all kinds of misfortunes, accidents, losses, and death.

West 7 Robbery and Evil Star (Metal Element): This unlucky star brings loss, robbery, violence, and gossip to the West sector.

The most important step in making Feng Shui work for you.

The Flying Stars make up 50% of helping you achieve your goals, but the remaining 50% is you identifying what you want to achieve and the actions you take.

Here are some of the examples on what you may want to see happen in 2022:

IDENTIFY YOUR GOALS FOR 2022

Here are some examples of what you may want to see happen in 2022...

- I want to start my own business and I am looking for investors
- I want to be in good health for 2022
- I want to find the courage to venture into new experiences
- I want to learn a new skill that can help increase my value
- I want to avoid any accidents or unforeseen circumstances
- I want to be indispensable to the company and secure my job
- I want to kick-start and create an additional source of income in 2022
- I want to grow my social media and gain more visibility

Based on your goal for 2022, you can activate the relevant sectors.

Based on your goals for 2022, you need to activate the relevant sector. To activate them, you must constantly carry out the appropriate activity in these areas. For example, do your work or make calls in the area - if you're ACTIVE here, you'll be one step closer to accomplishing your goals.

I want to meet the right people to help guide me in my endeavours.

1 Noble People

For goals related to looking for help, look for Flying Star 1 that's situated in the North sector this year. This place will be the perfect area for you to work, network, and make calls. It also helps you climb the career ladder.

I want to be in good health in 2022

2 Illness

If health is your main focus this year, you might want to avoid Flying Star 2 that's situated in the Southwest sector. This is because this star may amplify your health issues. If you're unable to avoid being in this area, you can place metal items here made out of brass, copper, bronze, or pewter.

I want to be have better relationships and have fewer arguments.

3 Arguments

To avoid arguments and misunderstandings, spend less time in the East sector of your house in 2022 as Flying Star 3 will be present there. That is because this star brings more harm than good within and invites a lot of conflicts. The key solution here is to have awareness and be more mindful of your words.

I want to learn a new skill that can help me increase my value.

4 Academic

In 2022, the Southeast sector will be occupied by the Flying Star 4. This auspicious star brings about inspiration and creative energy.

I want to avoid any accidents or unforeseen circumstances

5 Calamity

For a relatively smooth 2022 and to avoid any unforeseen accidents or injuries, avoid Flying Star 5 that's in the centre of the Flying Stars chart. If you really need to use this sector, it can be remedied with metal objects such as iron pots and copper cups (anything is fine as long as it is made out of metal).

I want to be indispensable to the company and get the promotion I want.

6 Career/Authority

If you wish to have authority, respect, and upward mobility at work, Flying Star 6 is what you need. Residing in Northwest this year, this star offers you a chance to climb the career ladder and your efforts will be noticed by the right people.

I want to strengthen my replationships with my family.

7 Discord

To avoid disagreements that may lead to a fallout with your family or loved ones, avoid Flying Star 7 that will be in the West sector this year. Do your best to not have any activities in this area as it might affect those who are married or in committed relationships too. Be prepared for a bumpy year ahead with the presence of this star.

I want to kickstart my sidegig and create an additional source of income in 2022.

8 Wealth

Want to grow your wealth or increase your income in 2022? Flying Star 8 that's residing in the Northeast sector is what you need. You should attempt to do all sorts of activities here such as brainstorming and financial planning to create the best results you want.

I want to find the courage to venture into financial investments and grow my profits.

9 Investment/Wealth

For those looking to grow your profit in terms of investment, look for Star 9 that'll be in the South sector. This is a very auspicious star especially for those of you who want to branch into financial investment or fund management. This is a good area for you to do your trading and investment planning

NORTH Front entrance
Annual Visiting Flying Star 1

For 2022 there will be the annual visiting **Flying Star 1**, Victory Star, known as the **Star of Triumph and Success**, in the North. This lucky Star is associated with winning, attaining success, reputation, good name, status, and fame. It brings triumphant victory over competition, career, and academic pursuits such as writing/research and scholastic success.

The Rat and North Sector will be receiving an abundance of help. You will be pleasantly surprised to find yourself surrounded by good people, some of whom can mentor you in personal growth as well as growth in wealth and career.

This lucky Star derives remarkable success for wealth opportunities, networking, and social circles, promoting reputation with influence and victory. Spending a lot of time in this vibrant sector of your home or office is beneficial for effectively enhancing your noble, wealth, and career pursuits.

The Flying Star 1 has a positive influence on attracting victory over past malaise and niggling health concerns. However, it is wise to watch out for emotional turbulences, such as emotional instability and depression. The Water element brings triumph to this Star, which you can activate by placing metal objects and/or a wind chime, water feature, Elephant, or a Victory Horse figurine.

According to the Bagua school of Feng Shui, this sector is representative of career and business, which you can enhance with the image of water, blue and black colours, and décor items. A Black Tortoise or Dragon Tortoise figure will also help in this area.

North Main Door Overview

Throughout this year, the Flying Star 1 will be in the North sector of the home. This is an advantageous position for you as there will be plenty of help emanating from this Star. Good people will surround you and many of them may even be able to help you grow.

All things can become smooth sailing; help can be gained from colleagues and even superiors. North Sector main door homes bring about advancement in business and career. You will be able to gain the recognition you want for everything you do. Achieving your professional goals is important, but what is more important is giving credit to those who aided you on your way to the top.

In addition to the numerous opportunities that exist with having your main door in the North sector of the home, it will also increase your likelihood of travel and growing your wealth. For 2022, Flying Star 1 will bring about guidance. Wise contacts will help you open the door to a whole new world, so be sure to listen. Profit and success could be nearer than you anticipate.

For couples looking to start a family, the Flying Star 1 is also a Star of importance. However, to best activate this Flying Star, land attributes such as a mountain need to be present. The ability to view a mountain or a hill from the North sector is a good sign. Conversely, having your main door close to highways or bodies of water may not be so lucky; instead, it increases your chances to face emotional issues, psychological complications, and even depression.

The month of April brings the monthly visiting Flying Star 5 (bad luck and obstacles).

The month of August has double Flying Stars in all sectors.

The month of July brings the monthly visiting Flying Star 2 (illness).

The month of June brings the monthly visiting Flying Star 3 (conflict, stress, and frustrations).

The month of February and November brings the monthly visiting Flying Star 7 (robbery).

SOUTHWEST Front entrance
Annual Visiting Flying Star 2

For 2022, there will be the annual visiting Illness **Flying Star 2**, which brings **sickness** to the Southwest of all homes and businesses.

Living under the same roof as the Flying Star 2 can be challenging to your health, particularly in areas relating to the skin and stomach. It is believed to worsen an existing illness. In 2022, matriarchal, elderly, and pregnant women residing in this sector of the home will be affected by this negative Star the most. It will affect you if your front door, main bedroom, or living area is located here. Goat and Monkey born people will experience feeling physically and mentally weak.

On the bright side, there are some benefits to having the Flying Star 2. For those dabbling in real estate and investment, this sector can be advantageous in bringing financial gain to your efforts. Having a Bright Hall outside your Main Door that is free from negative attributes can be greatly beneficial to you. It enables you to collect positive energy, bringing you positive property-related or real estate investment potential, but it will come at the cost of health.

It is strongly advised to help cure the Southwest of your home and business with a Buddha Vairocana amulet looking out, a Health Gourd (also known as a Wu Lou), six gold coins on a red tassel, a Saltwater Cure (page 80), and a Quan Yin. Metal wind chimes are not recommended; the Metal energy needs to be still and heavy, so metal wall sculptures work well instead. To counter the effects of this negative Star, you can place heavy Metal objects made of brass, copper, bronze, or pewter in this sector. Metallic artwork, colours, and home décor items are recommended to reduce and remove Fire and Earth energy.

According to the Bagua school of Feng Shui, this sector is representative of love, romance, and marriage. To enhance this, using a couple's image, pink peonies or a pair of Mandarin Ducks is recommended in this sector.

Southwest Main Door Overview

In 2022, the Flying Star 2, or also commonly known as the sickness and illness Star, is in the Southwest direction. Evident from its name, this Star will bring about health-related issues to those living within the home. To avoid activating the negative energies it carries, it would be best to not do any activities in the Southwest. Spend the least amount of time here. If your main door is unfortunately located in this area, you may want to look at other living options for the time being.

This can be a trying time, so be wise by watching the things you eat, working out regularly, drinking a lot of water, and getting plenty of rest. These steps will help minimize your chances of absorbing the negative effects of the Flying Star 2. Additionally, you should also regularly visit your doctor for check-ups. If you are a woman with child, make sure to avoid this area of the property altogether.

In addition to new health issues, this Star can also bring back old, pre-existing health issues. If you had something prior, be careful to keep all your medications within close reach. You and your loved ones should also be prepared for any sudden emergencies. To mitigate the negative effects of the Flying Star 2, fill this sector of your home with metal objects made from iron, bronze, copper, or brass.

Fortunately, this Star is not only bad - but it has also plus sides. For instance, it is a rather favourable star to have if you are into real estate and investments and will bring about financial gains and profits. To collect positive energy, you may want to create a Bright Hall right outside your main door, which might free your home from the negative attributes of the Flying Star 2. In conclusion, if your health is strong and you happen to be in certain industries, then your chances of winning throughout the year look good.

The month of May brings the monthly visiting Flying Star 5 (bad luck and obstacles).

The month of August has double Flying Stars in all sectors.

The month of August brings the monthly visiting Flying Star 2 (illness).

The month of July brings the monthly visiting Flying Star 3 (conflict, stress, and frustrations).

The month of March brings the monthly visiting Flying Star 7 (robbery).

EAST Front Entrance
Annual Visiting Flying Star 3

For 2022, there will be the annual visiting Quarrelsome **Flying Star 3** in the East sector. The Flying Star 3 brings conflict to the East, affecting those born in Rabbit years, those with bedrooms located East, and those whose homes have East-facing main doors. If not subdued, its quarrelsome energies can lead to lawsuits, court cases, and even jail time. As this Flying Star is the **conflict and dispute Star**, it is a hostile Star, known for bringing about violence, anger, misunderstandings, constant disagreements, heated arguments, litigation, trouble with authorities, and in extreme cases, legal complications between family members, friends, and/or colleagues.

Health issues related to the liver, gall bladder, feet, and arms may arise. Productivity will drop. If your bedroom is in the East, relationships between spouses will be affected by tense energies. Harmony of families and stability of marriages will be affected. Watch out for trouble with the authorities.

Women of the house and Rabbit-born people are the most likely to be affected. To avoid immediately activating the harmful negativity of the Flying Star 3, try to not use this sector of the home or avoid excessive movement and sound in the area.

Cures to be placed in the East sector include a red piece of paper, which is the traditional Chinese cure, or other red décor objects, rugs, candles, or bright lights. Nine Red Phoenixes can also be used, or the image of apples for peace.

If your front door is in the East sector, it would benefit you greatly to place Temple Lions there for extra protection along with an Evil Eye Symbol. Reduce Wood energy from the East for 2022.

Remove ALL wind chimes, bells, stereos, TVs, and musical instruments from the East rooms of your house.

According to the Bagua school of Feng Shui, the East is representative of health. Enhance with a Green Dragon and Quan Yin.

East Main Door Overview

For 2022, the Flying Star will sit at East main doors and in the East of your home. This Star may carry several negative effects; for example, relationship problems with the people around you. It could bring disruption to you throughout the year, but if you're smart, you also don't need to worry about it as much.

The troublemaker of Stars, the Flying Star 3 often causes disagreements to erupt between people. You may face arguments and backstabbing, bringing about unnecessary drama in your life. However, to know better and be better is a choice you can make for yourself. If you use your head instead of your emotions, then you may just avoid the conflicts which could arise.

The ability of this Star to cause problems in a relationship happens in different degrees. Regardless of the nature of those issues, you may just find yourself entangled in them anyway. These entanglements could involve legal problems or indirectly/directly getting caught in a lawsuit.

Your best move to make would be to leave this area of the house alone. This will, in turn, strengthen your relationships. Do not be worried if your main door is situated in this area, however, because this can be aided by placing a bright light to absorb the bad energy.

The month of August brings the monthly visiting Flying Star 5 bringing (bad luck and obstacles).

The month of August has double Flying Stars in all sectors.

The month of February and November brings the monthly visiting Flying Star 2 (illness).

The month of October brings the monthly visiting Flying Star 3 (conflict, stress, and frustrations).

The month of June brings the monthly visiting Flying Star 7 (robbery).

SOUTHEAST Front Entrance
Annual Visiting Flying Star 4

For 2022, the annual visiting Peach Blossom **Flying Star 4** brings **romance, academic, scholastic, and literacy luck** to the Southeast. It is called the Peach Blossom Star or a Star of beauty, knowledge, and learning. In 2022 it stands to benefit young women of the home, Dragon and Snake-born people. Generally, this Star brings about harmony and happiness in romantic relationships. It is highly auspicious for singles that are searching for love and marriage.

The Star brings about meaningful and fulfilling relationships. Those with a literary, artistic, or creative background, such as lecturers, teachers, artists, writers, and researchers, will see positive results in their work. Students using this sector will have better examination luck and luck in their applications for admission into good schools or universities.

To maintain and enhance love and romance in relationships, couples should strongly consider placing two Rose Quartz crystals next to or under their bed. You can also display love symbols, such as Mandarin Ducks, wish-fulfilling birds, or Huggers. To enhance academic luck, display the Chinese Saint Luohan or three Star Gods.

According to the Bagua School of Feng Shui, the South-East sector is governed by wealth and current cash flow. You can enhance wealth luck in this area with a water feature, Dragon Tortoise, and use any other wealth symbolism to strengthen.

Southeast Main Door Overview

Residing in the Southeast sector this year is the Flying Star 4, a star majoring in academics and arts. Priding itself in originality, if you're in these fields, then it will be a bright year indeed.

Having your main door positioned in this sector will indirectly help both artistic and creative energy to flow into the house. However, do not fret if it isn't, for you can also have a study/work room in this area as it can very much aid with reading, learning, and absorbing information. The Four Green will magnify abilities for occupants to do effective reading, to learn new skills, and to just grow as a person overall.

In addition to this, if you are a writer or a writer-in-progress, then you may want to spend time in this area of your property. Ghost-writers, copywriters, authors, or any other type of writer will flourish under the influence of this Star. Your best work may just come to you this year and you won't find yourself dealing with the inability to write or churn out ideas.

Makers, inventors, and crafters will also drink from the tap of the Flying star 4. Using your hands and your imagination in this sector could help you create things beyond your wildest imagination. You could end up blowing your very own mind with your extraordinary abilities.

The chance to travel the world again, or your dreams of going on a vacation abroad or visiting an exotic location, could be coming true this year. You will find yourself having good relationships with those around you and experience fewer relationship arguments, all thanks to the Flying Star 4.

The month of July brings the monthly visiting Flying Star 5 bringing (bad luck and obstacles).

The month of August has double Flying Stars in all sectors.

The month of October brings the monthly visiting Flying Star 2 (illness).

The month of September brings the monthly visiting Flying Star 3 (conflict, stress, and frustrations).

The month of May brings the monthly visiting Flying Star 7 (robbery).

CENTRE Annual Visiting Flying Star 5

2022 is ruled by the energy of 5: feeling free, self-emancipating, active, physical, impulsive, energetic, adventurous, resourceful, well-travelled, curious, excitement, change.

Environment with a 5 vibration is vibrant, alive, and everchanging. If you feel that you are stagnating in life, this is the perfect place for you for 5 is activity, movement, and change. Life becomes a merry-go-round of going to meetings, answering the phone, attending parties, and out-of-town trips. It is all exciting and adventurous. This is a good environment if you want to increase your communication skills. A 5 encourages a lot of people to come in and out; it is a hub of activity. 5 energy lends itself to mental stimulation, gathering information and experiences and sharing it - excellent for a journalist. A 5 lends itself to having experiences from a vast variety of areas. You might also think of a 5 house as a place for wine, women, men, and song, so if you are planning on being celibate, this is not the house for you. Your sexual appeal will increase with a 5 and romance will thrive.

Challenging aspects of a 5

Sometimes living in a 5 home can make you feel that your life is a whirlwind. Slow down and take time to smell the daisies. Also, there is sometimes a tendency to make snap decisions. Usually, your instincts are right in a 5 environment, but if it is an important decision, take a second breath and carefully deliberate before you decide.

For 2022, there will be the annual visiting **Flying Star 5** (also known as the Five Yellow Star) in the Centre, the most dangerous, vicious, and aggressive of all Stars. It is the **Star of danger, problems, bad luck, obstacles, calamities, and mishaps.** It is always bad news.

It affects all homes and households. Being an earth star located in an earth sector, this strong earth affliction cannot be ignored.

It is a malicious Star feared by all those wise in Feng Shui, as it tends to attract unfavourable outcomes, bad luck of all kinds and sometimes calamity. This can range from loss of money or salary to serious illness.

It is thought to cause major disruption in business plans, or even major accidents with serious injuries, which includes fatal accidents. When a bedroom resides in this area, it increases the effect of heart conditions and problems.

There are many damaging manifestations, like bankruptcy, betrayals, disloyalty, obstacles, tragedies, mishaps, and anything else that is negative, depressing, or hazardous. This area should be avoided completely where possible. Parties and activities are a big no-no. Avoid playing loud music or having a television on. Those born in Dog, Dragon, Ox, or Goat years should be mindful.

Do not attempt renovation projects, drilling, or wall breaking in the centre of a home or sector or a room located in the centre during this time. Keep this sector as quiet as possible to avoid energizing this star.

The most effective way to combat the 5 Star is to leave it alone to the best of your ability – do not disturb it! If that is not possible, it can be pacified with a Brass Pagoda along with a Saltwater Cure.

To counter the effects of this negative Star, you can place heavy Metal objects made of brass, copper, bronze, or pewter in this sector. Metallic artwork, colours, and home décor items will also reduce the effects of Flying star 5 and remove Fire and earth energy.

The month of August brings the monthly visiting Flying Star 5 (bad luck and obstacles).

The month of August has double Flying Stars in all sectors.

The month of February brings the monthly visiting Flying Star 2 (illness).

The month of January and October brings the monthly visiting Flying Star 3 (conflict, stress, and frustrations).

The month of June brings the monthly visiting Flying Star 7 (robbery).

NORTHWEST Front Entrance
Annual Visiting Flying Star 6

The Northwest represents the luck of the Patriarch and is the home sector of the Dog and Pig.

For 2022, there will be the annual visiting Heavenly **Flying Star 6,** a **Star bringing speculative, windfall heaven luck** poised to bring good fortune, blessing the Northwest sector and encouraging manifestation of career prospects. It is said to bring power, status, authority, good name, and prosperity luck as well as career luck straight from heaven.

It is also known as an indirect wealth Star of good luck, also straight from heaven, that bodes well for professional activities, especially if you want to climb the career ladder or achieve higher recognition at work. Enhanced status and authority, good name and reputation are indicated in this Star. This is especially good news for the patriarch. Boost the Flying star 6 auspicious metal energies and enhance for CEOs, bosses, leaders, and patriarchs' ability to lead.

The authority that is brought upon by the positive aspects of this Star can also indicate status and influence in social circles. The home influence will be most dramatic and will also benefit from this heavenly Star.

As both the Dragon and Tiger together symbolises wealth luck, displaying images of Dragons in years of the Tiger becomes even more auspicious. Bring life to the Flying star with yang energy, such as a water feature, metal, sound, and activity. Traditional enhancers include a Horse figurine, six gold coins on a tassel, or gold ingots.

If activated by negative external forms, the lucky 6 can turn abruptly and bring with its sudden upheavals, changes, and medical complications to the kidney or legs.

According to the Bagua school of Feng Shui, this sector is representative of mentors and helpful people. This sector is also representative of the head of the household and signifies influential benefactors which can be enhanced with metal décor items or the three Star Gods. The Star Gods also represent health, wealth, longevity, and are beneficial in the main living area of a home.

Northwest Main Door Overview

The Flying Star 6 this year will occupy the Northwest sector of your home. Its position will help attain rewards, recognition, as well as career growth.

If your home has a Northwest main door, then its positive energy will further be magnified into various aspects of your life. All your workplace efforts will finally come to fruition and you will be able to bask in the benefits.

The energy from the Flying star 6 may also aid you in any long-time quest for a promotion. The power and authority from this Star will provide the chance to be appreciated by management.

If you work in the sectors of tourism, printing, freight-related businesses, military, academia or sports, the Northwest direction will prove most beneficial. This isn't, however, to say that those who are not in these fields will not be rewarded. Good opportunities and success will certainly follow the lot of you throughout the year with this star. Do keep in mind though, there are still certain negative aspects to this star, for instance, problems at the workplace and health complications (legs/kidneys). Nevertheless, these can only be activated with negative features in the sector.

The month of September brings the monthly visiting Flying Star 5 (bad luck and obstacles).

The month of August has double Flying Stars in all sectors.

The month of February brings the monthly visiting Flying Star 3 (conflict, stress, and frustrations).

The month of March brings the monthly visiting Flying Star 2 (illness).

The month of July brings the monthly visiting Flying Star 7 (robbery).

Lucky Bamboo is associated with wealth, good luck and wellbeing. Bamboo is symbol of prosperity, good fortune, success and longevity. Lucky bamboo can be given as a gift so that others can have better luck, health, and abundance. When a lucky bamboo plant is gifted, make sure the right number of stalks are tied as each number of stalks have different meanings, five stalks represent good mental and physical health while 3 stalks provide good luck, long life and plenty of wealth. 3 stalks is often used as a cure for the flying star 7.

WEST Front Entrance
Annual Visiting Flying Star 7

For 2022, there will be the annual visiting **Flying Star 7**, an inauspicious **Robbery and Evil Star** taking refuge in the West. The Flying Star 7 is very feared because of the potential of theft, burglary, and violence

The West will mainly have an adverse effect on emotional and physical wellbeing.

In 2022, those who use the West sector of their home a lot will find themselves embroiled in drama that will likely be caused by misunderstandings.

Office politics and competitions will be high. Being swindled by others is a real possibility. Watch your back during this period and be careful who you trust.

Strong emotions, robbery, gossip, and villains can be averted if you steer clear of the West.

Sickness related to the mouth and teeth may surface. There is the possibility of hospitalisation or surgery for those with existing health complications. Remedy this Star with the traditional cure of three pieces of Bamboo in a transparent glass vase of water in the West, the Evil Eye symbol with seven glass elephants, or place one blue rhinoceros and one blue elephant or a pair of Blue Rhinoceros figurines in this sector. You can also place the anti-burglary door guardians or the anti-burglary and anti-violence image facing out of the home.

A water feature also helps to exhaust the Metal energy of the Flying Star 7.

Flying Star 7 especially affects the young woman, lady, daughter, and Rooster born occupants.

According to the Bagua school of Feng Shui, this area is representative of descendants, family, children, and the protection of your current assets and wealth. You can place any wealth symbolism in this area to assist such as gold coins, gold ingots, a Wealth Bowl, God and/or a Dragon Tortoise.

West Main Door Overview

The Flying Star 7 in the West this year is not a good sign for those in relationships because this area of the home will bring about a lot of drama and misunderstandings between two people. This Star is known to cause tension in relationships and disrupt proper communication. Should your bedroom be situated in the West of your home, you may want to prepare yourself. If possible, do as little as you can in this sector and try moving your sleeping area elsewhere.

Regarding health, this Star may also set some unwanted notions in motion. If you are one with pre-existing health conditions, then the Flying star 7 may aggravate it so your best move would be to be aware of your health. Do not only become concerned with your body when you detect a problem; instead, be on full alert from the get-go. Stay fit and keep healthy, with exercise regimens as well as a balanced diet.

Bad news may arise if your main door is situated in the West sector of your home because the positioning may increase your chances of getting robbed or having thieves steal from you. Be extra vigilant of your possessions and place extra locks on your doors.

If you find lamp posts or sharp roof corners pointing to the West, then you must be careful. This is because these objects may indirectly bring harm to your personal well-being and your career. It could set off a series of negative events, derailing both of those chapters in your life. Conversely, having hills that are visible from the West of your home is a positive sign. This may symbolise that there are noble people who will always be ready to help, should you ever find yourself in need of it.

The month of January brings the monthly visiting Flying Star 5 (bad luck and obstacles).

The month of August has double Flying Stars in all sectors.

The month of April brings the monthly visiting Flying Star 2 (illness).

The month of March brings the monthly visiting Flying Star 3 (conflict, stress, and frustrations).

The month of August brings the monthly visiting Flying Star 7 (robbery).

NORTHEAST Front Entrance
Annual Visiting Flying Star 8

For 2022, there will be the annual visiting **Flying Star 8** shining brightly over the Northeast sector, making it the luckiest sector of the year. It is the **Star of wealth, finance, new income, and current prosperity,** bringing abundance, money, fortune, good luck, nobility, and steadfastness. You can expect improved income, success, and power luck.

Professional pursuits, a good reputation, and efforts acknowledged will flourish if you can tap into this positive sector.

If you are lucky enough to have the Main Door in the Northeast sector, good energy will be ushered into your house, bringing blessings and positive news. There is a strong chance that you will be able to see these benefits from the wealth sector materialise with increases to your income. Financially you will thrive, and you can further enhance this by keeping close tabs on your investment portfolio. There will be a significant surge in activity here that will require wise decision-making. Additionally, this auspicious sector is very beneficial for employees who have their eyes on the goal of being promoted or getting a pay raise.

To allow energy to flow, this area should be kept clutter-free. To activate its luck, any form of wealth symbolism can be placed in this area, such as a Buddha, 6 gold coins on a tassel, a Wealth God, or gold ingots as well as bright lights clocks, TV, and lots of activity.

This Star is especially timely for Ox- and Tiger-born, as well as boys of the home.

According to the Bagua School of Feng Shui, the North-East is representative of knowledge learning and education, which you can enhance with a world globe or world map.

Northeast Main Door Overview

For 2022, the Northeast will be the wealth sector of the property with the Flying star 8 residing. Should your main door be in the Northeast, then it will be a good year with prosperity and great fortune.

Flying Star 8 ushers in only favourable blessings and great news. You will be able to reap the benefits of the wealth sector in more ways than one. There could be an increase in your income or you may find yourself receiving profitable gains via your investments. You will do well financially and your best bet during this time would be to keep a close eye on your investment portfolio. You may need to rethink how to manage it properly for the best benefits.

With regards to your career, this will be a year of pay raises, golden opportunities, recognition, and advancement. If you have set your focus on being promoted or getting an increment, 2022 will be when it happens for you. Besides that, you may also find yourself with interesting choices this year, so be sure to grab opportunities that present themselves without hesitation. If you are seeking recognition, step up in your field and prove to your superiors what you're made of. Credit will be given where credit is due.

If you do not have your main door in the Northeast sector, merely place a small water feature in the Northeast. This will energize the Flying Star 8 and allow you to absorb all its goodness. Placing Yang-natured items, like clocks, fans, and televisions, may also be an alternative if a water feature isn't possible. Use this sector of your home to its maximum capacity, perhaps as an activity room, as it will bring about some amazing effects to your life.

The month of February and November brings the monthly visiting Flying Star 5 (bad luck and obstacles).

The month of August has double Flying Stars in all sectors.

The month of May brings the monthly visiting Flying Star 2 (illness).

The month of April brings the monthly visiting Flying Star 3 (conflict, stress, and frustrations).

The month of September brings the monthly visiting Flying Star 7 (robbery).

SOUTH Front Entrance
Annual Visiting Flying Star 9

For 2022 there will be the annual visiting **Flying Star 9** shining brightly over the South.

It is the **Star of Completion, magnification and Future Prosperity,** happiness, and recognition. This dynamic and entertaining Fire Star spurs celebrations, festivities, gatherings, and excellent luck. It is referred to as the Star of Completion because it shows the ability to bring successful fruition to projects that were started previously. It affects success in finance and abundance luck, enhancing the luck to have a positive outcome in the future from the seeds you have previously sown.

It is also a secondary Star that brings wealth, boosts business, increases profits. and benefits investments. Inhabitants in the South will be seeing overall mass improvements to their wealth, luck, and relationships, both social and romantic. Maximise the effects of this sector to its full potential and you will find yourself in a better position than last year in more aspects than one. This Star has the potential of bringing an increase to your income, especially to those already under steady employment. If you fall into this category, this sector is also beneficial to those who are contemplating a career change or starting a new relationship

The Horse and teen girls are more likely to enjoy these good influences and will be inclined to experience victory luck in competitive activities.

This Star boosts fame and recognition. You are advised to use this space frequently if you wish to start a new business, plan to marry, or intend on starting a family. Enhance with any wealth symbolism such as Buddha, a trinity of horses, 9 gold coins on a tassel, a Wealth God or gold ingots, objects in multiples of nine, (for example, nine golden dragons) or a Red Phoenix. Keep this part of the home or office brightly lit and lots of red upholstery and decor are encouraged here.

According to the Bagua school of Feng Shui, this sector is representative of fame, recognition, and reputation. Along with a Horse statue, a Red Phoenix would be most auspicious in this area to benefit this Feng Shui school.

South Main Door Overview

If there are any sectors to be maximized this year, it is the South of your home. If your main door is in the South, you will certainly have a good year ahead. Improvements to wealth, luck, and all forms of relationships will happen.

With regards to career, if you have a steady, long-time job you will see a potential salary raise. An increase in your income can certainly be something you can look forward to. Conversely, if you are looking to change careers or start a new relationship with someone, this year would also be a favourable year to do so.

Activating the South main door will also mean activating a more creative, expressive side to you. You may find yourself coming to light with your numerous skills and the ability to produce perfect work. Recognition and rewards will come flowing due to this.

In terms of relationships, whether romantic, platonic, or familial, the Flying star 9 proves rather fruitful. Should you have ideas of building a strong relationship with another, the South would be the place to be in. Spend a ton of time here and you will be able to absorb all the positive energy emanating from the Flying Star 9.

Getting married or building a family are also good moves to make in 2022. If you are single and not looking to have any intimacy, do not fret, for even platonic bonds have been predicted to flourish with this Star.

The month of March brings the monthly visiting Flying Star 5 (bad luck and obstacles).

The month of August has double Flying Stars in all sectors.

The month of June brings the monthly visiting Flying Star 2 (illness).

The month of May brings the monthly visiting Flying Star 3 (conflict, stress, and frustrations).

The month of October brings the monthly visiting Flying Star 7 (robbery).

HOW TO MAKE A SALTWATER CURE

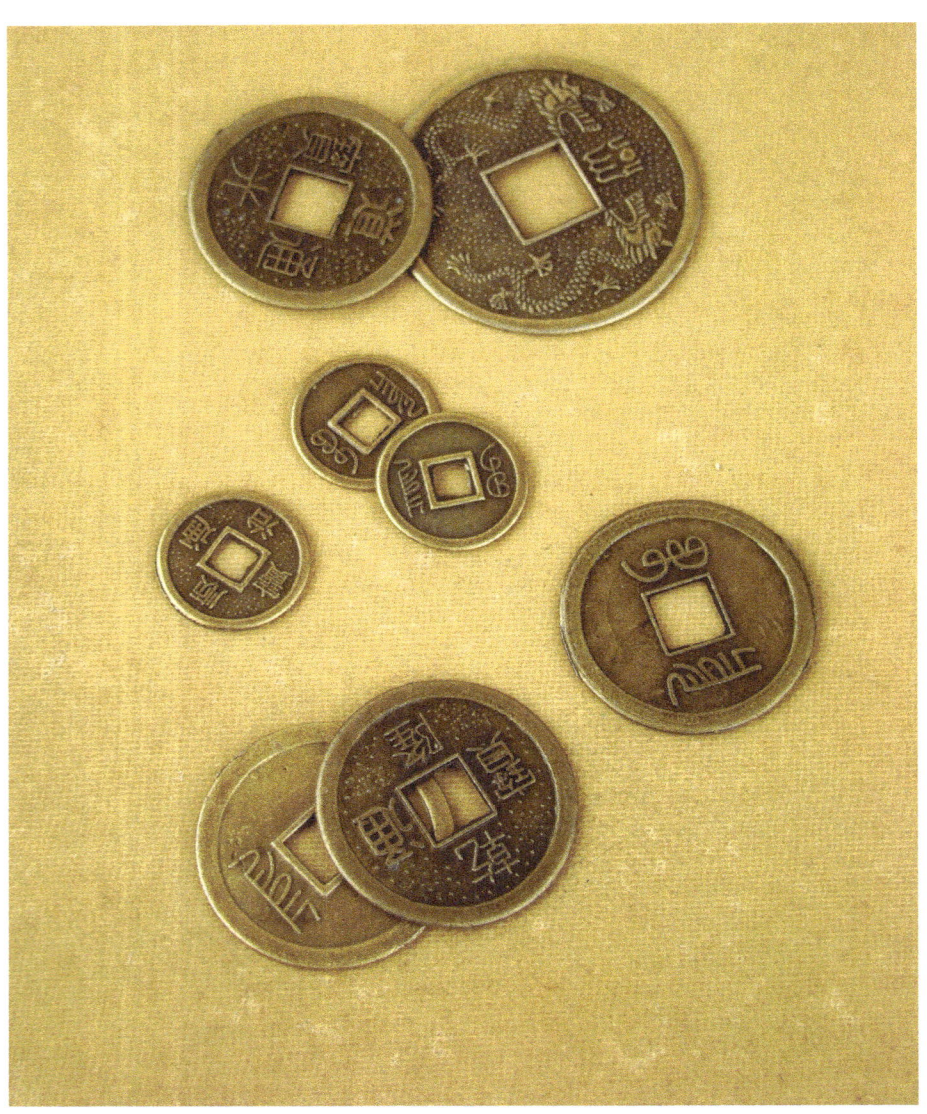

Items you need.

- Salt (Saxa rock salt)
- A container (glass, porcelain, or metal), Pint glass or jar
- Six Chinese Coins (made from brass) or six coins
- Water (to fill your chosen container)
- A protective mat or a stand.

Step-by-step instructions

1. Fill your chosen container with salt up to ¾ or the top of its capacity.
2. Place the six coins on top of the salt; the coins should place with the Yang side up (the side with the four Chinese characters) or heads up.
3. Add water to fill the container to the top.
4. Place the container on a protective mat or stand in the area where you need it.
5. The saltwater cure container should be left open. Do not cover it or place it in a covered space such as a cupboard.

Placement suggestions

Place your Saltwater Cure in an area where you know the container will be safe (i.e., not tipped over, moved, or otherwise tampered with). Usually, a corner in the room works well.

If you do not like the look of the Saltwater Cure (it will change even more in time), be sure to place it behind a decor object so that it is not visible. For example, you can have your Saltwater Cure behind the sofa, a screen, or a big, lush plant. You should have access to it to add water as needed.

It is normally used in tandem with other Metal cures because the ill effects of the Flying Stars 2, 3 and 5 are destroyed by Metal. Feng Shui cures, such as a Brass Pagoda, Health Gourd, and Six Gold Coins on a red tassel, are often used together with a Saltwater Cure to achieve the best results.

How to dispose of your Saltwater Cure

The Saltwater Cure will absorb and accumulate a lot of negative energy, so care should be taken with its disposal. **Do not cleanse** the bowl and the coins as **the whole cure needs to be discarded**. Simply wrap it in newspaper and discard it in your rubbish bin.

ANNUAL VISITING FLYING STARS
Afflictions

The energy in your home and office changes from year to year. Therefore, it is necessary to take care of these shifts.

Flying Stars is a school of Feng Shui. The annual visiting Flying Stars are believed to be the most powerful elements of Feng Shui. Each year, the Flying Stars change their positions around February the 4th, the beginning of spring in China. Auspicious and affliction Stars fly into new sectors of a home or building, reflecting changes in energy to each of the locations.

To maintain good Feng Shui and a smooth transition into the New Year, it is important to take note of the locations of each Star. Each year also brings monthly visiting Flying Stars into each sector of a home or building. While the annual visiting Flying Stars are more significant, it is also important to note the sector changes due to monthly visiting Flying Stars.

Knowing the positions of these Stars allows you to install appropriate cures and remedies to afflicted areas and efficiently activate the good fortune areas by placing the correct enhancers and activators.

Each year a couple of major energies impacts us...

Grand Duke - Tai Sui / Sui Po / Three Killings / Year Breaker / The Five Yellow

GRAND DUKE - Tai Sui

Northeast 3 52.6° - 67.5°

In 2022, the Grand Duke flies into the Northeast 3 sector of your property. Avoid aggravating the negative energies of this star by disturbing this sector, either through renovation or ground-breaking. Potential accidents and catastrophes are likely if the Grand Duke is activated, and there are also serious implications of medical problems. It would not be good to face the Northeast 3 direction during work or even during major work discussions and meetings. It would be best to try to put your back towards this direction, as that will enable you to regain the upper hand in professional negotiations and all career-related activities / projects.

Why DO we pay attention to the location of the Grand Duke - Tai Sui?

The Tai Sui, or God of the Year, is said to oversee all matters that take place on Earth. It is important to gain his support while making sure one does not inadvertently incur his wrath. His movement mirrors that of the planet Jupiter, hence he is sometimes also known as "Grand Duke Jupiter".

The Grand Duke -Tai Sui in Astrology

In Chinese Astrology, it is believed that when the Tai Sui enters your animal sign location, you are blessed with good fortune as the Tai Sui is said to support your sign. This is known as "sharing the space" with the Tai Sui. However, if your animal sign location is directly <u>opposite</u> the Tai Sui's position, the sign is said to be "confronting" the Tai Sui, which brings afflictive energy. The animal signs that are located ninety degrees from the Tai Sui's location are said to be in "side clash" with the Tai Sui. This is referred to as "Sui Po" and is directly opposite Tai Sui. Sui Po tends to bring challenges, obstacles, and can affect your health. It can force you to **change and adapt**. That can mean a **new beginning, opportunity, or direction in life**. It can be a turning point.

Those born under animal signs with any kind of clash with the Tai Sui need to make a special effort to appease the Tai Sui for that year. For those confronting the Tai Sui, it is advised to display his image in the home in his location for the year.

In 2022, the **Monkey** is in direct clash with the Tai Sui.

The **Tiger**, the animal sign for this year, is being backed by the Tai Sui. However, because of its proximity to the Tai Sui, those born under the Tiger sign are also advised to pay homage to him to ensure his support continues throughout the year.

So, in 2022, it is suggested for **Tiger, Snake, Monkey, and Pig** to display the Grand Duke – Tai Sui in the NE sector of their homes.

The Grand Duke - Tai Sui in Feng Shui

In Feng Shui, we are always mindful of the location of the Grand Duke -Tai Sui for the year. In 2022, the Tai Sui's location is **Northeast.** It is advised to have the Pi Yao in the NE in 2022 as this heavenly creature is the best symbol for appeasing the Grand Duke - Tai Sui.

Facing the Grand Duke - Tai Sui direction is also not favourable. If your work desk is facing Northeast, you should adjust your desk to face a different direction this year.

DO NOT FACE NORTHEAST this year EVEN if the NE happens to be one of your "good" directions under the KUA formula.

Every year, the direction of Tai Sui is considered the superior or monarch position, which opposes the subject or inferior position. The opposite direction of Tai Sui (Sui Po Direction, or the direction of Year Breaker) is known as conflict with Tai Sui, which means the subject will offend its monarch. In Feng Shui theory, it is a top taboo to conflict, clash, or damage Tai Sui. The directions in conflict with Tai Sui are as follows:

1. A door opposite the direction of Tai Sui. If the door of your office or room is facing the direction of Tai Sui or the opposite, it is a clash with Tai Sui.

2. Layout. If your seat, bed, office, kitchen, or bedroom faces away from Tai Sui or the opposite direction, it is a clash with Tai Sui.

3. Break ground. It is a taboo to break ground in the direction of Tai Sui or the opposite direction. Otherwise, you will offend Tai Sui and invite misfortune.

In addition, you will clash with Tai Sui if you attend school, engage in trade, work, or travel in the direction of Tai Sui or the opposite.

THREE KILLINGS

North 337.6° - 22.5°

This year, the Three Killings is in the North sector. Make sure you do not sit with your back to the North instead, you should confront and face sitting North. Preferably, this area should be left alone and remain undisturbed throughout the year, especially not be activated for ground-breaking or renovations. Otherwise, you may risk causing some serious negative consequences for the property itself and its inhabitants. Potential repercussions include mishaps and accidents, robberies, theft, loss of wealth, and material possessions. As well as persistent health troubles and complications, the traditional solution is to place strong Plant or Earth energy of crystals in the **North** to exhaust three killings.

So as an example, what you cannot do to give you a better idea of how the Three Killings can be disturbed:

- Installing a pond or swimming pool – not advised
- Using a main door in the North – not advised
- Replacing windows or doors in the North – not advised
- Play drums in the North as loud as you possibly can – not advised
- Drilling into walls (single holes for hanging pictures should be fine) – not advised
- Lay a new patio or deck – not advised

YEAR BREAKER

Southwest 3 232.6° - 247.5°

It would be best to avoid all forms of renovation or ground-breaking works in this sector to avoid incurring any negative consequences. The Year Breaker is also sometimes referred to as the "Wrath of the Grand Duke". Disturbing the Year Breaker or aggravating it in any way may lead to serious repercussions with outcomes that could be worse than the ones triggered by the Grand Duke.

HO TU SPECIAL 2022
AUSPICIOUS STAR COMBINATIONS

The exciting, auspicious phenomenon of this year's Feng Shui chart is the presence of four "HO TU" special combinations that bring extra kinds of luck. Activating the Ho Tus sectors will unlock good fortune! Generally, Ho Tu Specials benefit the sector in which they occur and will benefit those living in these sectors, or those whose animal signs are in these locations. When all four combinations appear in the chart, everyone in the Zodiac can gain from them if all four combinations are activated in the house.

Some of you may have extra luck this year to balance out the negative energies. 2022 has hidden Ho Tu combinations, which can manifest as good luck, windfalls, and victories.

According to Feng Shui theory, Ho Tu numbers are four pairs of numbers placed in a certain manner in the Flying Star chart.

They are representations of the Yin and Yang energy combinations of the five elements and only fall into specific patterns occasionally. They can be either positive or extremely negative.

The Ho Tu numbers must fall into primary cardinal directions to form these combinations:

- 1-6 falling in the North (representing the Water element)
- 2-7 falling in the South (representing the Earth element)
- 3-8 falling in the East (representing the Wood element)
- 4-9 falling in the West (representing the Fire element).

In 2022 all four Ho Tu number combinations appear in all annual Flying Star charts. As all of them happen to be positive, it will bring better luck to the Rat, Horse, Rooster, Ox, and Tiger.

As they are in the South, North, West, and Northeast, this means that Chinese Astrology birth signs, associated with each of these sectors, have a greater chance to improve luck in the area associated with their sector.

North for example, is the Rat's home sector and it is associated with commercial or business luck.

This means in 2022, if you are born in the sign of the Horse, you can expect recognition and to be noticed due to the South.

If born in the sign of the Rat, expect either good luck associated with your career or business due to the North.

If you are the sign of the Rooster, you can expect heavenly luck and assistance due to the West.

And if you are born in the sign of the Ox or Tiger you can expect good academic achievements from the Northeast.

The 1 - 6 Ho Tu brings SUPERIOR INTELLIGENCE to those needing to make important decisions.

Sitting in the North and Northwest, the Ho Tu brings strong luck associated with learning.

Anyone engaged in literary and academic pursuits benefit from activating the 1 - 6 Ho Tu in the North and Northwest! It especially benefits the Rat, Pig, and Dog.

The 4 - 9 Ho Tu brings BIG PROFIT LUCK to those pursuing commercial ventures.

Big business success sitting in Southeast and South bring luck associated with commercial success!

This Ho Tu brings strong benefits to the Dragon, Snake, and Horse.

The 3 - 8 Ho Tu brings LEADERSHIP luck to those in positions of power.
Sitting in the East and Northeast, power and growth bring political luck and new power.

It is highly recommended for the Rabbit, Tiger, and Ox and those whose bedrooms, entrances, and living rooms are in the East or Northeast.

The 2 - 7 Ho Tu brings ASSET WEALTH luck for your investments and your net worth.

Lucky for Rooster, Monkey and Goat.

The 2 - 7 Ho Tu combination triggers the luck of big money to the West and Southwest, helping to offset other negative stars here.

BAGUA Aspects for 2022

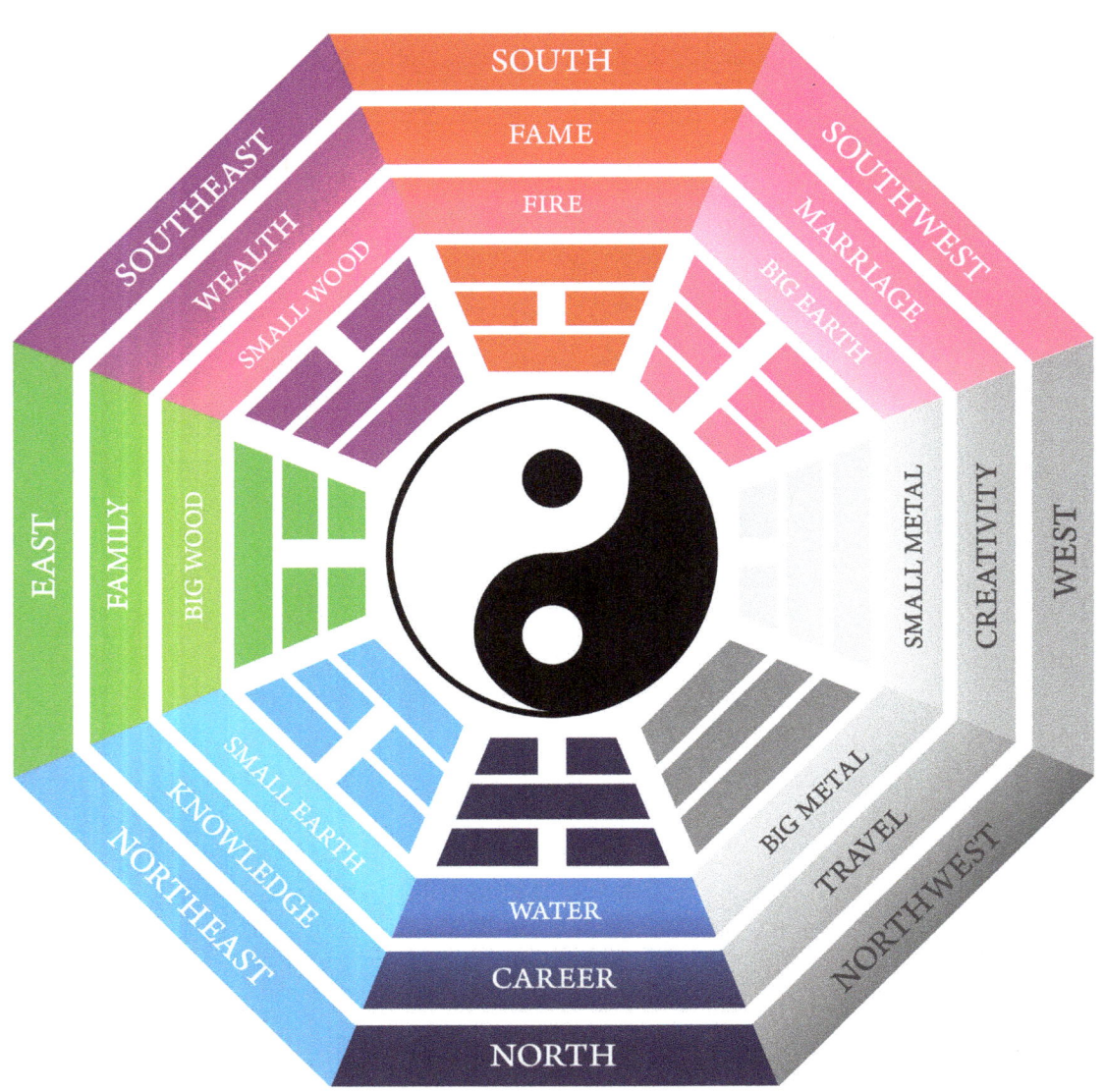

South - fame and recognition for 2022

The Flying Star 9 is dynamic. It enhances a positive outcome for the seeds you are sowing and encourages endeavours towards boosting new enterprise, income, marriage, and births. It brings especially good luck for teen girls in 2022.

This secondary wealth Star also brings a magnifying and multiplying influence on luck. The positive energy of this Flying Star brings new beginnings, new ventures, and happy events. You should use the rooms in this sector frequently if you wish to start a new business, plan to marry, or want to start a family.

Make sure that you place a statue or a picture of the Horse and or Phoenix in this sector to increase your opportunities of success with lots of red upholstery and decor here.

Southwest - relationships, love, and romance for 2022

Due to the negative Annual Flying Star 2, which represents sickness and ill health over this sector for 2022, there may be persistent health problems, sickness, and malaise. The occupants of a house facing Southwest or with the main door located in the Southwest sector will be more vulnerable to digestive system illness (stomach, pancreas, and spleen) and miscarriage. It will mostly be the mother, Grandmother, or eldest female of the building.

It's important that pregnant women stay away from this area completely if possible. Move to another bedroom or if that's not possible, use Feng Shui cures to subdue this Star's aggravating health issues. Suppress the illness energy of this Star with Wood and Metal, or six gold Coins and a Wu Lou tied with a red ribbon or a Metal Health Gourd. A Quan Yin, six rod Windchime, or the saltwater cure will also help.

As this sector relates to love and relationship luck, it is very important that the Southwest and or Southeast pocket of the master bedroom and family areas are enhanced with lucky relationship symbols such as happy family or couple photos, the Double Happiness Symbol or Mandarin Ducks.

West - wealth and prosperity for 2022

Due to the Annual Flying Star 7 being over this sector for 2022, there could be issues to do with money and perhaps finance related legal problems. Be careful of betrayal, gossip, and backstabbing within the family. It especially affects the youngest son and people who spend a lot of time here. Temperamental emotions, robbery, and gossip can be averted if you steer clear of this sector. Unhealthy competition in your workplace is also indicated. There may be sickness related to the mouth and teeth.

Remedy this Star with the traditional solution by placing three pieces of Bamboo plant in a clear glass vase of water in the West location. Also helpful are a pair of Blue Rhinoceros figurines on both sides of the doors to this sector, or the Evil Eye and Elephant Feng Shui cure figurines. These Feng Shui cures are strong protective symbols will weaken the Metal energy of this Flying Star when also including Water element. If your main door is located here, it's even more important for you to take safety precautions. If this is your front door place, a Bagua mirror on the outside for protection will help.

Northwest - helpful people and mentors for 2022

Due to the positive Annual Flying Star 6 being over this sector for 2022, you will see improvement and good fortune.

This Flying Star is associated with the energies of heaven. It is a very favourable good luck Star that bodes well for a good name and professional activities, especially if you want to climb the career ladder or achieve higher recognition at work. The Flying Star 6 is a Star of advancement, windfall luck, power, and authority if you can spend a lot of time in this part of your house or office and activate the energy. There can also be an increase of enhanced scholarly luck, status and authority, good name, and reputation luck. Males of the family will find its influence the most dramatic. Selling a home will be easier this year if facing Northwest.

Bring life to this Star with Yang energy, activating sound and activity in this corner by placing a figurine pair of Elephants to increase and strengthen descendent luck. This Flying Star's element is Metal, so enhance it with Metal or Earth (crystal) energy. Traditional enhancers include six gold Coins or a six rod Metal Windchime. Also make sure that you place a water feature or a picture of water in this area.

To support the patriarch and mentor luck, place a Kwan Kung or Fuk Luk Sau in the sector. Remove anything associated with Fire energy and moving objects such as a fan and television. Have no gatherings or noisy activities here. Do not have open fires or bright lights and use another entrance (if possible). Keep doors and windows closed and avoid any construction or renovation in this area. Exhaust the Earth energy of the five with Metal energy based on the five-element weakening cycle. A pagoda, six rod Windchime, or the saltwater cure will help subdue this Flying Star.

North - career and business for 2022

Due to the positive Annual Flying Star 1 being over this sector for 2022, this aspect will see much improvement for relationships.

Lucky Flying Star 1 can help you attain victory over competition and enhances career promotion and monetary growth. Relationships, knowledge, wisdom, romance luck, creativity, learning, and study will be a lot easier. This Flying Star will benefit the middle son of the house most but is also associated with career and business.

Spending a lot of time in this vibrant North sector of your home or office this year will enhance your pursuits and wealth or career-related endeavours. It is the Water element that brings triumph and luck. You can activate this auspicious Star by placing a water feature, a picture of water or a Metal Windchime in this sector to increase your opportunities of success. A bowl of water with blue stones and a small statue of a Turtle can be used, or for success, a Metal Horse or the Dragon Tortoise can be used in your home or office.

Northeast - education and knowledge for 2022

Due to the positive Annual Flying Star 8 being over this sector for 2022, gaining recognition and acknowledgement will be quite easy and rewarding.

The Flying Star 8 represents current prosperity, so this sector of your residence or office is very favourable. The youngest son of the family can expect to see positive benefits. It is the Star of fortune and good luck and brings with it prosperity, wealth luck and steadfastness.

If your home has a main door, living or family area in this sector, everyone in your home will gain from this Star. You can expect some good financial returns and strong career advancement.

It is an Earth element and can be activated with Feng Shui crystals or enhancers related to the figure eight such as the infinity or mystic knot symbols. Any form of wealth symbolism can be placed in this area as well as bright lights and lots of activity. Try to leave the door open and use this area as much as possible.

East - health for 2022

Due to the negative Annual Flying Star 3 being over this sector for 2022, family issues will be affected this year. There could be arguments, conflict, anger, frustrations, and stress to do with family, your work, staff, and clients.

It will affect mostly the first-born son and those sleeping in this sector will find themselves easily stressed and agitated. Health issues related to the liver, gall bladder, foot, and arms may arise. Feng Shui cures to be placed in the East sector include a piece of red paper, rug, pillows, bedspread, candles or bright lights. The Fire energy of these cures is crucial to incinerate the Wood energy of this Star. If your main door or family room is located here, it affects everyone in the household. Place a Buddha, pair of Fu Dogs or Temple Lions to safeguard you. Place red Fire energy at your workplace to protect yourself from back-stabbing and rumour mongering. If you can't display the cures, try to remove Water or Wood energy from this sector.

Southeast - family and wealth luck for 2022

Due to the positive Annual Flying Star 4 being over this sector for 2022, which improves romantic opportunities and study and literary fortune for writers and scholars.

The Flying Star 4 brings romance, scholastic and literacy luck to the Southeast. It is also often called the Peach Blossom Star or a Star of beauty, knowledge and learning. In 2022, it stands to benefit teenage girls of the home, and Dragon and Snake-born people. Generally, this Star brings about harmony and happiness in romantic relationships.

Those with a literary, artistic or creative background such as lecturers, teachers, artists, writers and researchers will see positive results in their work, with indication of further advancement. Students using this sector will have better examination luck and better luck.

The South-East sector is governed by wealth, current cash flow. You can enhance wealth luck in this area with a water feature, Dragon Tortoise and any other wealth symbolism to strengthen.

As this area is represented by the Wood element, so use lots of plants and flowers. Water gives life to Wood, so by using small water features or pictures of water you can also activate this section.

GLOSSARY

Arowana - a popular wealth symbol often used in Feng Shui. The Arowana is considered a highly intelligent fish that is associated with being able to foresee negative events. It can emit strong vibrations when it senses danger is near. It represents generations of wealth and the pacifying of negative forces. It is displayed for career luck and in the Water element area in Flying Stars, so place in North for 2022.

Bagua - also called Ba-gua or Pakua is one of the main tools used in Feng Shui to analyse the energy of any given space, home, office, or garden. It is a powerful form of protection for your home or business. The trigrams are arranged in the potent heavenly sequence to protect you, your home and business from negative influences. They should never be placed within the home or business, as it is too strong a cure for inside the premises. Rather, place them on the outside of the home or business facing out. When placing, make sure that it is not being blocked by pillars, columns, or the roofline/eaves. Translated from Chinese, Bagua literally means eight areas.

Bells - make a beautiful sound and are sensitive to any form of movement, making them a useful Feng Shui cure. For thousands of years Bells have been symbolic of warding off negative influences, and the announcement of goodwill.

Brass Windchimes - are used for the Metal element to assist in counteracting the negative effects of the Flying Star 5. Use also in the Northwest section for helpful people and mentors.

Coins - ancient Chinese Coins have been used as a Feng Shui cure for many thousands of years. They symbolize wealth and are representative of the Metal element, so they can be used in areas that require this. When placing your Coins, ensure that they have the side that has the four Chinese characters facing up, this is the Yang side which is more active than the side with the two Chinese characters, which is the Yin side and is more passive.

Double Happiness Stand - this symbol represents long lasting love and strong relationships. It may be placed in the Southwest section of the bedroom or in the Southwest section of the house or office/business.

Dragon - is one of the celestial animals in Feng Shui. A symbol of strength, courage, and endurance. Place on the left-hand side as you look out of the home or the East section of a building or room to assist in the health area.

Dragon Tortoise - is a celestial creature said to be a hybrid of the celestial Dragon with the sturdy and steadfast Tortoise and is displayed by many Feng Shui practitioners to bring great fortune to their homes or workplaces.

The Dragon Headed Tortoise is a powerful symbol attracting support, wealth, and good luck. Dragon and success, and the Tortoise's longevity of tenure, ensures a long and successful career. It is a must have if you are in the business or a cutthroat corporate environment. The Dragon Tortoise is also a fantastic energizer for scholastic finesse and superior knowledge.

Elephant - the Elephant is the symbol of strength, wisdom and prudence. It symbolizes the year and is thus a celestial animal in Buddhism. It is sacred because it was said to offer flowers to Buddha and carries the gem of wishes and the sacred alms bowl of Buddha. Together with the Tiger, Leopard and the Lion, the Elephant is one of the four creatures that represent the power of energy.

Five Element Pagoda - encompassing the five essential elements of Feng Shui, this pagoda can be used to ward off negative Earth energies and of Flying Star 5.

Flaming Magic Wheel - represents the Fire element, which is associated with recognition and career. Being one of the eight auspicious symbols of the path to enlightenment, it is considered a wonderful symbol of protection against negative gossip and legal mazes. The Flaming Magic wheel may be placed so it is visible on one's business desk to represent flowing dealings with all people in the workplace. In Flying Stars Feng Shui, it is placed in the argumentative Flying Star 3.

Fu Lu Shou or Fuk Luk Sau - These three wise men (or Star Gods), are the most sacred of all Feng Shui deities as they represent health, wealth, and longevity.

Horse - the seventh sign of the Chinese Zodiac; in Chinese Feng Shui it symbolizes perseverance and strength. Horse figurines in your home or workplace will strengthen and enhance all the good traits and characteristics it represents in family members born in the year of Horse. It is no surprise that you can almost always find paintings and sculptures of horses in Chinese homes and businesses. In Feng Shui, the horses are usually classified into Tribute Horse and Victory Horse. Place in the South to enhance your reputation and to receive recognition.

Mandarin Ducks - come in pairs and are excellent symbols of keeping your love life alive. They are said to be a potent symbol of love and marital bliss as they create Chi that helps lovers tie the knot. Anyone wanting to energize their love life, should place them in the in the Southwest sector of your bedroom, side by side as equals. They must always be placed together, facing in, and never apart.

Mystic Knot with Evil Eye amulet - has no beginning and no end and represents never ending food fortune. The Evil Eye represents protection against jealousy and malicious intent by reflecting it back to the sender. It can be placed in the home, workplace, or cart.

Pi Xiu or Pi Yao - a mythical creature of purity, loyalty, abundance, and protection. The delightful Pi Xiu is said to be a loyal friend who always looks after its owner. Place on your work desk, in the Southeast for wealth, or at your front entrance or family room.

Precious Gourd - also known as the Health Gourd or Brass Wu Lu, is an ancient Chinese symbol of longevity, protection from illness and negative energy. It can be used for promoting good health. Hang from the head of the bed or behind door. A wonderful talisman to take for travel protection.

Prosperity Symbol - is a replica of the ancient Chinese Ingot; the shape being like a boat representing abundance and an easy life. It may be placed in the Southeast section of the home, office or room for attracting wealth; the West for assisting the protection of wealth luck or in the Northwest section for encouraging mentors and helpful people.

Quan Yin - is sometimes known as the female Buddha, Goddess of mercy and compassion, however, she is a Goddess within her own right. She assists in deflecting conflict, arguments, disruptive issues, illness and sickness. She is also the protector of children. Quan Yin is best placed where there a disruptive issue like in a sickroom, a child's room, and open plan offices. Note though, never place Quan Yin directly on the floor or in negative rooms such as toilets, bathrooms or laundries.

Row of six I Ching Coins - these Coins are used to weaken the Flying Star 2.

Temple Lions or Fu Dogs - guards you from poison arrows, negative people from entering your home and used when the 'robbery' Flying Star is located at the entrance of your premises. It's very popular in many Asian countries outside. The Male is playing with a ball. He symbolizes authority, courage and command. The Female has her claw on her cub, for protection and loyalty. Place at your front entrance, facing out with the Male on the left and the Female on the right.

Victory Banner - used for success, love, and protection. Containing the three powerful symbols of protection, the Victory Banner represents wisdom over ignorance.

CANDLE SPACE CLEARING

Candle space clearing is a simple technique used to clear stagnant, stale or bad energy in a home. It can be done when you first move into a home, after an argument, to revitalise from poor health, or whenever you feel the need.

To clear space in your home, light one tea light candle in each room situated such that each candle can 'see' at least one other candle. Rooms such as bathrooms, toilets, walk-in-robs are included.

A statement to say when lighting each candle.

> "I ASK THE UNIVERSAL GOD TO PLEASE BLESS THIS HOME (OR BUSINESS).
>
> PLEASE RELEASE ALL NEGATIVE ENERGY SUCH AS ANGER, SADNESS, SICKNESS, LOSS, FEAR, ETC.
>
> PLEASE BRING INTO THIS BUILDING SUCCESS, HAPPINESS, WEALTH, EXCELLENT HEALTH, KNOWLEDGE, ABUNDANCE, JOY AND LOVE.
>
> PLEASE RELEASE ALL SPIRITS FROM MY HOME (OR BUSINESS)."

TIPS

- Allow the candles to burn down completely
- Burn uplifting oils, (pure Sandalwood or White Sage are great)
- Play gentle music and follow recommendations made in your personal report.

BEGINNERS FENG SHUI
'EASY TIPS TO ENHANCE EVERYDAY LIVING'

A beginner's guide to learning the fundamentals of Feng Shui and energy flow in the home, known as Chi. This ancient art of placement brings balance, helps to improve the harmony and prosperity within your space. Ideal as a gift for the novice wanting to learn more or beautiful coffee table book to inspire you on your next home renovation.

Buy Beginners Feng Shui   www.completefengshui.com

Ebook Beginners Feng Shui   www.completefengshui.com

COMPLETE FENG SHUI NEWS IS FOR YOU - TO NAVIGATE AND UNDERSTAND YOURSELF AND ENVIRONMENT:

Monthly Subscription

- Monthly Feng Shui and Flying Star Outlook
- All 12 Animals Chinese Horoscope Forecasts and Day Masters
- Calendar Auspicious date selection… And much, much more
- Over 40 pages to navigate monthly Feng Shui

Subscribe   **www.completefengshui.com**

COURSES / WORKSHOPS

- 2022 Complete Lifestyle Retreat
- Understanding Feng Shui and your home
- Landform and Symbolism… making the most of your home and interior
- Show Me the Money – Chinese Astrology for Career, Wealth and Success
- Lifestyle Feng Shui – Better Living with Feng Shui
- Good Feng Shui… Property and Real Estate
- Getting to Know YOU, Beginners Chinese Astrology Part 1 & 2
- Module 1: Health, Wealth & Prosperity
- Module 2: Four Pillars of Destiny Part 1 & 2
- Module 3: Flying Stars Part 1 & 2
- Module 4: Practitioners Course and Business Practices for a Feng Shui Business
- Feng Shui Refresher workshop

ABOUT
Michele Castle

Michele has been in demand as a Feng Shui consultant for nearly two decades. Trained by Master Raymond Lo of Hong Kong, Juliana Abraham Feng Shui Centre in Perth, Western Australia, and has studied with Dato Joey Yap and Lillian Too. Michele maintains her Master studies each year to ensure she continues to provide clients with the best of her skills. Michele has an uncanny ability to read charts and has a fantastic insight into people. She combines experience and natural intuition with the multi-layered discipline of Feng Shui, to deliver positive outcomes for clients. Michele's approach is practical, realistic and simple. She adores the reward of making a difference in the lives of her valued clients.

Having studied architectural drafting and interior design and working with interiors and renovations on her own homes it was a natural progression to incorporate Feng Shui and metaphysical studies into those projects. Applauded for her style, Michele was often asked if she could share her gift with others. Passion and dedication, combined with further studies, saw her first Feng Shui business, Energize Life Feng Shui born and evolve into Complete Feng Shui.

Michele conducts onsite Feng Shui consultations for residential and corporate clients. An accredited teacher, at recognised training institutes, author and public speaker with numerous radio and television guest appearances. Michele works alongside families, with residential homes, developers, architects, interior designers, real estate agents, restaurants, cafes, day spas and retail stores.

For any existing or proposed business client Michele can help with staff recruitment, choosing the best location and orientation for business premises, improving the atmosphere and working environment, and advisement on business stationery such as letterheads and business cards.

For the residential client, Michele offers guidance on how to improve health and harmony in the home, how to choose the best home for you and how to improve the chances of selling your home. Other services include how to choose a suitable career for children or elderly family members and how to improve children's behavior, sleep and studies.

Michele's practice and qualifications include Classical, Form, 8 Mansions, 24 Mountain Compass, Flying Star School Feng Shui. Site selection and design. Metaphysical studies of Four Pillars of Destiny / Bazi / Pa Chee, Qi Men, Millionaires Feng Shui with special interest and studies on Feng Shui Love and relationship luck.

Michele teaches beginner to practitioner Feng Shui seminars, workshops, courses and retreats, as well as conducting on-site learning experiences at homes and businesses. Students receive complete course notes. For those who have mastered the basics of Feng Shui and wish to continue their studies and share their knowledge with others, there are courses to explore.

With an ability to relate to people from all walks of life. Based in Perth, but regularly consulting in UK, South Africa, Malaysia, Singapore, Bali and eastern states of Australia on residential, business, and commercial properties.

Author

Beginners Feng Shui – Easy tips to enhance everyday life
365 Everyday Feng Shui Tips Journal
Complete Feng Shui Monthly Planner 2022
Complete Feng Shui Diary 2022 – Year of Water Tiger

Michele truly believes.

" Life is what our thoughts environment and energy make it".
"Change your environment and thoughts, change your life".

With the knowledge of Feng Shui, it can work to increase wealth, enhance health, and harmonise relationships.

Beginners Feng shui 'Easy tips to enhance everyday living'

A beginner's guide to learning the fundamentals of Feng Shui and energy flow in the home, known as Chi. This ancient art of placement which brings balance, helps to improve the harmony and prosperity within your space. Ideal as a gift for the novice wanting to learn more or beautiful coffee table book to inspire you on your next home renovation.

Beginners Feng Shui www.completefengshui.com

365 Everyday Tips Journal 'Easy Tips to follow to enhance everyday life'

www.completefengshui.com

Complete Feng shui '2022 Monthly Planner'

www.completefengshui.com

Complete Feng shui '2022 Diary'

www.completefengshui.com

Complete Feng shui DAILY FORECAST

daily date selection, actions, tips and luck for YOU

daily forecast www.completefengshui.com

"Feng Shui Today

Day of Metal Goat

Good day for Rabbit and Pig, a day to act.

Not so good day for Ox, a day for Ox to lay low to avoid challenges

A day to be Stable.

Conflict direction is West.

A day suitable for Ground-breaking, Getting married, Meetings, Renovations, Signing contracts.

Suits Rabbit, Horse, Goat, Pig.

Average for Rat, Tiger, Dragon, Monkey, Dog.

Bad – Avoid major decisions and activities if Ox, Snake, Rooster.

Today's Flying Star is **Flying Star** *5 Misfortune and Obstacles Star (Earth Element) also known as Wu Wang or 5 Yellow Star: It is considered the most malevolent and dangerous of the nine Stars, it brings all kinds of misfortunes, accidents, losses and death.*

Today's Tip

Develop sensitivity to your surroundings. Good Feng Shui practice requires the ability to spot secret poison arrows in the surrounding environment These arrows hurt you only when they are pointed directly at your front door.

www.ingramcontent.com/pod-product-compliance
Lightning Source LLC
Chambersburg PA
CBHW061805290426
44109CB00031B/2941